MARK RAINSLEY

PADDLE THE SEVERN

A GUIDE FOR CANOES, KAYAKS AND SUPS

First published 2023

Published in Great Britain 2023 by Pesda Press
Tan y Coed Canol
Ceunant
Caernarfon
Gwynedd
LL55 4RN

Copyright ©2023 Mark Rainsley

ISBN 9781906095895

The author asserts the moral right to be identified as the author of this work.

All rights reserved. No part of this publication may be reproduced, stored in a retrieval system, or transmitted, in any form or by any means, electronic, mechanical, photocopying, recording or otherwise, without the prior written permission of the publisher.

Contains Ordnance Survey data © Crown copyright and database right 2023

Maps by Bute Cartographic

Printed and bound in Poland, www.hussarbooks.pl

Below Apley Forge.

Foreword

My first paddling experience of the River Severn was in 2018. I spent three days on her, paddling the wrong way. I'd innocently believed a friend who had told me that I wouldn't notice the flow of the river against me. I didn't really, until each time I stopped and was swiftly whisked downstream. This was part of my Land's End to John O'Groats SUP expedition. I'd never really done any river paddling before; I was an ocean lover through and through. But for 200 miles of my 1000-mile journey from one end of the UK to the other, I chose to paddle on canals and rivers, to follow plastic's journey from our lives inland to the ocean I love so much.

I knew I had only scratched the surface and despite a lot of my three days feeling like I was walking up a 'down' escalator, I wanted to return one day and paddle the rest – in the right direction. So, in 2020, as soon as we were released from lockdown and into the wilds, I came back to get to know her better.

The UK's longest river, steeped in history and myth, begins with a humble trickle in the Welsh hills. It isn't long before, in the Hafren Forest, she's already roaring over boulders, creating immense waterfalls and supporting stunning and dense nature along her banks, from enormous trees to tiny dragonflies. She's wild from the word go.

My plan was to paddle from the first navigable section of the river out to sea over a couple of weeks. I pushed out from the banks at Crewgreen, and for days I was awed by the ever-changing scenery. Fields of livestock gave way to impressive towering red rock, and as I paddled silently through these canyons, I could have believed that I was somewhere much more exotic than Shropshire. There was evidence of our industrial history at Ironbridge, juxtaposed with untameable rapids at Jackfield. I saw my first ever kingfisher; a bright blue streak darting across in front of me, then another, and another. Squirrels climbed enormous trees on the banks and crows settled into their riverside roosts for the evening.

As the river winds her way through towns and cities, she changes again. She becomes the centre-point of life. People connecting with nature on her banks, floating downstream on boats, feet dangling in the water whilst sat with a pint on a riverside pub pontoon. One day, I had the joy of sharing my experience with some wonderful people for whom the river is a lifeline for their mental health. The passion for this body of water follows her wherever she weaves.

The estuarine section of the River Severn is different again; fast flowing and fiercely tidal. The Bristol Channel opens out and stretches ahead, reminding us of how, all along the river's length, all the water, all the wildlife, and all these people are inherently connected to the ocean.

My trip down the length of the River Severn was to highlight exactly this; that we all have a stake in the health of our rivers and ocean, and in return a responsibility and ability to look after them. But first, that drive to protect a place comes from falling in love with it. I hope you fall in love with the River Severn, just as I did. And if you're planning an A to B paddle, I highly recommend paddling downstream.

Cal Major

OCEAN ADVOCATE, FOUNDER OF THE SEAFUL CHARITY

WWW.CALMAJOR.COM

WWW.SEAFUL.ORG.UK

Cal Major.

Contents

Foreword 4
Contents 6
Introduction 8
About the Author 9
Acknowledgements 10
Disclaimer 11

Severn Highlights 13

The River Severn 17
An overview of the Severn 17
Climate and flows 20

Planning your Journey 23
Who? 23
When? 23
Which paddlecraft? 23
Carrying gear 25
Safety 25
Seeking help 30
Water levels 31
Locks 31
Expeditions 32

Which bank? 37
Grading white water 37
The Severn Way 38
Maps 39

Access to the Severn 41
Pool Quay to the sea 41
Above Pool Quay 42
Responsibilities 42
Further information 43

The Severn Uplands 44
The Source 47
Section 1 – Severn-Break-its-Neck Waterfall to Llanidloes 51
Section 2 – Llanidloes to Llandinam 57
Section 3 – Llandinam to Newtown 63
Section 4 – Newtown to Garthmyl 69
Section 5 – Garthmyl to Pool Quay 75
Section 6 – Pool Quay to Montford Bridge ... 83
Section 7 – Montford Bridge to Shrewsbury 91

The Middle Severn 99
Section 8 – Shrewsbury to Ironbridge 101
Section 9 – Ironbridge to Bridgnorth 111
Section 10 – Bridgnorth to Bewdley 121
Section 11 – Bewdley to Holt Fleet 131

The Severn Vale 139
Section 12 – Holt Fleet to Severn Stoke 141
Section 13 – Severn Stoke to Tewkesbury 151
Section 14 – Tewkesbury to Gloucester ... 159
Section 15 – Gloucester to Sharpness 169

The Severn Bore 181
About the Bore 181
Viewing the Bore 182
Surfing the Bore 183
Further information 185

Launching on the Severn 187
Launch points 188

Camping 193
Campsites 194

Culture and Landscape: The Story of the River Severn 201
Geology 201
History 203

Wildlife and Environment 215
Environmental issues 215
Habitats 217
Wildlife 220

Further Reading 226
Useful books 226
Historical sources 227

Index 228

Introduction

"Apart from its historic associations or from its interest purely from the canoeist's point of view, the River Severn is one of the finest rivers in England from its source to its mouth, traversing some of the finest scenery which these islands have to offer."

Alec R. Ellis, *The Book of Canoeing*, 1935

My dad and I launched our kayaks into the River Severn above Ironbridge; mine was a fibreglass torpedo, his was a more graceful wooden affair with a wobbly v-shaped hull. Nanoseconds later, we emerged from the Ironbridge Gorge at Coalport Bridge, wide-eyed and breathless: we hadn't realised that the Severn was flowing high! The river flushed us through the gorge's (seemingly) towering waves with breath-taking rapidity, but despite our inexperience had the good grace to deposit us upright and safe at the end. Nearly four decades later, we repeated the trip in a double canoe; dad boringly insisted on hopping out and walking around the main rapids.

The River Severn offers so much to canoeists, kayakers and paddleboarders. Britain's longest river accommodates the needs of touring, competitive and expeditioning paddlers (as well as those simply 'bimbling'), with room to spare. Paddlers can choose between the river's diverse but always attractive and engaging surroundings; Cambrian Mountains white water, North Shropshire Plain meanders, deep Midlands valleys, broad Worcestershire flood plains, expanses of estuarine sandflats. Several things may surprise paddlers uninitiated to the Severn; it is clean, green and lush, its ecosystems healthier than they have been in centuries; it is remarkably quiet and free of traffic; and finally (perhaps most surprising of all) it is untamed and free-flowing with white water along its length, only engineered in its final freshwater stretches. The Severn's human history has been shaped by its course through the borderlands between England and Wales, but equally by its continual importance as a trade route. Folk from prehistoric times onwards have left traces accessible to paddlers, from cathedrals and castles to quaysides and canals. Most famously, Ironbridge was 'the cradle of the Industrial Revolution' with its Iron Bridge proudly recalling these epochal developments. If you do nothing else on the River Severn, at least paddle beneath the bridge!

This is the first paddling guidebook to the River Severn which covers the entire river in all its moods. This book aims to guide paddlers along the Severn and through its rapids, riffles and locks, whilst also highlighting the river's natural and historical surrounds. I hope that it helps you to enjoy some great adventures on this long and lovely river.

Mark Rainsley

About the Author

Mark Rainsley

Mark has spent over three decades using paddlesport as a means of avoiding adulthood and responsibility. He is a fanatical paddler who has descended challenging white-water rivers worldwide, and who is dedicated to exploring every nook and cranny of the UK's coast and rivers by canoe, kayak and paddleboard. He is a prolific contributor to paddlesport magazines and other media. Mark has authored numerous Pesda Press guidebooks including *South West Sea Kayaking*, *Paddle the Wye*, *Paddle the Thames* and *Paddle Shakespeare's Avon*.

The author.

Acknowledgements

A big thanks to the numerous paddling friends and family who joined me in exploring the length of the River Severn during 'research' for this book!

I'm hugely grateful to the following folk, who helped create this book; Cal Major was kind enough to write the foreword. Paul Robertson outlined his experiences surfing the Bore. Lotte and Peter Johns described their source-to-sea expedition. Jenna Sanders offered advice on Duke of Edinburgh Award expeditions. Bill Taylor supplied his experiences of the Severn's wildlife. Dr Lizzie Garnett offered input on geology.

Finally, thanks to Franco Ferrero at Pesda Press, Vicky Barlow for her great design work and Don Williams of Bute Cartographic for the stunning maps, and Andrew Whiting and Kath Goodey for their proofreading skills.

Photographs

All photographs by Mark Rainsley, except where acknowledged in the captions.

Maisemore Weir.

Important notice – disclaimer

Canoeing, kayaking and other paddlesports, whether in a river or sea environment, have their inherent risks, as do all adventurous activities. This guidebook highlights some considerations to take into account when planning your own river journey.

Whilst we have included a range of factors to consider, you will need to plan your own journey and within that ensure there is scope to be adaptable to local conditions; for example, weather conditions and ever-changing river hazards (especially weirs!). This requires knowing your own abilities, then applying your own risk assessment to the conditions that you may encounter. The varying environmental conditions along the Severn mean that good judgement is required to decide whether to paddle or not.

The information within this book has been well researched. However, neither the author nor Pesda Press can be held responsible for any decision of whether to paddle or not and any consequences arising from that decision.

Jackfield Rapids.

Severn Highlights

We hope that this book will inspire you to explore and enjoy as much of this wonderful river as possible. However, here are just a few suggested highlights to get you started ...

Nature untamed

Places of natural beauty to enjoy from the water or (where public access exists) via forays on shore.

- Hafren Forest (The Source)
- Dolydd Hafren nature reserve (Section 5)
- The Isle (Section 7)
- Attingham Park estate (Section 8)
- Severn Valley Country Park (Section 10)
- Seckley Wood and Wyre Forest (Section 10)
- Lincomb Lock (Section 11)
- Longney Sands and the Noose (Section 15)

Industrial heritage

Legacy sites which evoke the Severn's past of trade, transport and industry.

- The Montgomery Canal (Section 4)
- The Iron Bridge, Jackfield and Coalport (Section 9)
- The Severn Valley Railway (Section 10)
- Bewdley's Georgian waterfront (Section 10)
- Stourport Basins (Section 11)
- Upper Lode Lock (Section 13)
- Upton-upon-Severn's waterfront (Section 13)
- The Gloucester and Sharpness Canal (Section 15)

White water excitement

Rapids and riffles for beginners to experts.

- All of section 1!
- Above Dolwen Bridge (Section 2)
- Severn Bridge Rapids (Section 3)
- Cil Gwrgan Bridge (Section 4)
- Preston Boats Weir (Section 8)
- Ironbridge Gorge and Jackfield Rapids (Section 9)
- Bridgnorth to Hampton (Section 10)
- Folly Point Rapids (Section 10)

Hills and high points

Enjoy these landmarks from the river, or ascend them for a bit of perspective.

- Plynlimon (The Source)
- Yr Allt Gethin (Section 2)
- Breidden Hill and Rodney's Pillar (Section 6)
- The Wrekin, Wenlock Edge and Ironbridge Gorge (Section 8)
- Quatford's cliffs (Section 10)
- Pendlestone Rock and High Rock (Section 9)
- Wainlode Hill (Section 14)
- Garden Cliff, Newnham and Hock Cliff (Section 15)

Worcester Cathedral.

History and culture

Engaging historical and cultural sites along the river's course, to appreciate from the water or visit separately.

- Dolforwyn Castle (Section 4)
- Powis Castle (Section 5)
- Atcham Bridge and St Eata's Church (Section 8)
- Wroxeter Roman City / Viroconium (Section 8)
- Buildwas Abbey (Section 8)
- Bridgnorth High Town (Section 10)
- Worcester Cathedral (Section 12)
- Odda's Chapel and Ashleworth Tithe Barn (Section 14)

The Wrekin.

The River Severn

*"There is a gentle nymph not far from hence,
That with moist curb sways the smooth Severn stream:
Sabrina is her name."*

John Milton, *Comus*, 1634

An overview of the Severn

The River Severn is the longest river in the United Kingdom, and the second longest in the British Isles; Ireland's River Shannon is several kilometres longer. The river's 'official' length is 354km / 220 miles; the author measures it as two kilometres shorter. It's all subjective though, as the end point is simply an arbitrary line (identified in the twelfth century by writer Giraldus of Wales) across saltwater between Severn Beach / English Stones and Bedwin Sands at Sudbrook, which nowadays intersects with the five kilometre-long Second Severn Crossing bridge. The river's start point is much easier to pin down, being a boggy pool on a mountain in mid-Wales. The two spots are just 124km apart; the Severn takes a roundabout and leisurely route to the Bristol Channel. It passes through four counties; Powys in Wales, then Shropshire, Worcestershire and Gloucestershire in England. The Welsh Severn, called the Hafren, begins as a mountain river which descends 480m in the first 25km. The remaining 130 metres of descent to sea level is spread along 255km. The surprising thing (at least, to those used to heavily engineered rivers such as the Thames) is how freely and swiftly the water flows along that length. The majority of the Severn was never tamed, remaining *"still in a state of nature"*, as John Randall put it in 1880. Only a smattering of weirs hinder the river's flow; riffles and even white-water rapids (often around islands known as bylets, eyots or naights) are a commonplace feature all the way downstream to Stourport-on-Severn in Gloucestershire. Here, the 68km-long Severn Navigation commences.

In this book, the river has been divided into three parts: the Severn Uplands, the Middle Severn and the Severn Vale. These are the administrative names used by the Environment Agency, which conveniently highlight the river's distinct incarnations as it makes its way from mountains to sea.

The Severn Uplands

"This natural part of the river offers something of interest all the way. Rapids and hazards are evenly spaced. Anyone with moderate experience who is willing to inspect anything doubtful should have an enjoyable trip."

Percy Blandford, *Canoeing Waters*, 1966

The River Severn, or Afon Hafren in Welsh, emerges at 610m above sea level on the sprawling mountain of Plynlimon in the Cambrian Mountains. The same mountain gives rise to the Rivers Wye and Rheidol. The source of the river is easily accessible to walkers and the uppermost sections can be tackled by white-water paddlers. The river passes through the market towns of Llanidloes, Newtown and Welshpool, growing from accumulated tributaries; the white-water

📷 *Below Moel-lart.*

rapids are interspersed with broad or braided stretches, sprawling unhindered across the flood plain with wonderful mountain views. The river counter-intuitively narrows as it trends north-east across the Marches (the historic English / Welsh border area) via a mind-bending succession of bends and switchbacks.

📷 *Above Llandinam (literally). Photo | James Appleton.*

High Rock, Bridgnorth.

The Middle Severn

*"The steeple vanes of Shrewsbury dream
… And the memory of her mountain springs
Is all forgotten – for now in sooth
She floweth mantled in her sober state."*

Francis Brett Young, *The Island*, 1944

From the town of Shrewsbury, the now-sizeable and mature river ambles languorously across a huge plain formed by an ancient glacial lake bed, before regaining power and purpose at Wenlock Edge. It narrows to breach this barrier of hills, with vigorous rapids through Ironbridge Gorge. The rapids continue as the now south-flowing river wends between the enclosing hills and red sandstone cliffs of Shropshire and then Worcester's Wyre Forest, demarcating the Midlands' western edge. This is a stretch of exceptional natural beauty and even remoteness, despite, or possibly because of, the industrial heritage recalled by the former ports at Ironbridge, Bridgnorth, Bewdley and Stourport-on-Severn. From this latter town downstream, the locks and weirs of the Severn Navigation tame the river.

The bends above Buildwas.

The Severn Vale

"The very water of the Severn, like that of the Nile, impregnates the valley ... all the country is so fruitful, wherever this river does overflow, and its waters reach."

Daniel Defoe, *A Tour Through the Whole Island of Great Britain*, 1725

Between the historic cities of Worcester and Gloucester, the Severn Navigation's river traffic is surprisingly light and the river passes through idyllic countryside, lined by greenery and with views of the Malvern and Cotswold Hills. The River Avon joins at Tewkesbury and the Severn enters the Vale of Gloucester, a broad plain of wide flood-meadows known locally as Hams. The Vale of Berkeley below Gloucester hosts a dramatically different River Severn, the powerful and intimidating tidal reaches infamous for the Severn Bore. This remarkable landscape is accessible to paddlers with appropriate experience and competence. In this book, the river is described as far as the port of Sharpness; the final kilometres passing below the Severn Road Bridge to the river's supposed end at the Second Severn Crossing involve some very serious sea kayaking challenges.

Climate and flows

The Severn drains 11,422 square kilometres, not including the flow of its tributaries the River Wye and Bristol Avon which join in the tidal reaches. There are at least 25 other tributaries, of which the largest are the Vyrnwy, Teme and Warwickshire Avon ('Shakespeare's Avon'). At the source on Plynlimon, average annual rainfall measures 2,058 mm, falling on around 200 days; the river never runs dry! Rainfall decreases along the length of the river to just 339mm at Haw Bridge, before rising again to 769mm at Gloucester, influenced by the sea's proximity.

Apart from rainfall, the Severn's flow is affected by releases from Llyn Clywedog and Lake Vyrnwy. The Afon Clywedog was dammed in the 1960s, partly to regulate the Severn's flows. Water is released in dry periods, augmenting the Severn near its source at Llanidloes and maintaining a minimum flow of 10 cumecs (cubic metres per second) at Bewdley. Releases are also made before exceptionally high tides, to deter saltwater from reaching Gloucester's drinking water supply. Although releases are held back after heavy rainfall, this has negligible impact in terms of flood control. At Dolwen Bridge, just 23km from the source, the Severn's mean flow is 6.5 cumecs. It reaches a healthy 15 cumecs by Brynderwen Bridge and at Montford Bridge,

Above Haw Bridge.

Sabrina

The river has been called Severn / Hafren / Sabrina, all seem to be variations on the same name. Severn derives from the Latin name Sabrina, first used to describe the river by Tacitus and Ptolemy in the second century AD. This name might mean 'sandy' or possibly 'summer fallow land'. The Welsh version may be the oldest; Hafren is Celtic, possibly meaning a 'boundary' or perhaps from *afon* (river) and *frenhines* (queen). It's also possible that all the names are simply variations on the Celtic *abona / afon / avon*: river.

Geoffrey of Monmouth took the name's obscure origins and invented the legend of Sabrina in his 1136 *Historia Regum Britanniae* (History of the Kings of Britain), a pseudohistory in which most of the King Arthur stories originated. Geoffrey told how Queen Gwendolen commanded her innocent and pure step-daughter, *"to be thrown into the river now called the Severn ... So that to this day the river is called in the British tongue Sabren, which by the corruption of the name is in another language Sabrina"*. Monmouth's drowned girl was the love child of Celtic / British nobles and Germanic invaders, symbolising the river's frontier nature.

In John Milton's 1634 masque *Comus*, Sabrina, *"underwent a quick immortal change, Made Goddess of the River"* and as a river deity, *"sways the smooth Severn stream."*. Sabrina is represented in various artistic interpretations along the river; carvings in Llanidloes park and on Worcester Bridge, statues beside Bridgnorth Castle and in Shrewsbury's Quarry Park.

towards the end of the Severn Uplands, it is 43 cumecs. The mean flow at Bewdley on the Middle Severn is 61 cumecs and at Haw Bridge in the Severn Vale, the mean flow is 105 cumecs. A flow of 105 cumecs equates to a little over nine billion litres passing beneath the bridge daily and makes the Severn the most voluminous river in England and Wales; only Scotland's River Tay carries more water in the UK. The highest recorded flow on the Severn was a staggering 1,400 cumecs*, at the peak of the summer 2007 floods. The Severn is famously prone to flooding, with the most severe impacts typically experienced in the Severn Vale. The river's sorry history of flood events is outlined on page 213.

* *The flow gauges were overwhelmed, so this figure was extrapolated / guesstimated by the Environment Agency.*

Below Apley Forge.

Planning your Journey

"The longest and noblest of Britain's streams is still an unexplored river ..."

Brian Waters, *Severn Stream*, 1949

This section is intended to outline the factors involved in paddling on the Severn, whether you plan to splash about for simple fun, or whether you have grand expedition plans.

Who?

The Severn is suitable for and accessible to all ages, genders and abilities. Complete beginners or novices will find a perfect environment for learning and progressing quickly, provided they plan appropriately and take due care around locks and weirs. The Severn Uplands, upstream of Pool Quay, are recommended for more experienced paddlers with understanding of how to tackle challenges and hazards such as trees, portages and white-water rapids. The tidal parts of the Severn Vale downstream of Gloucester are only recommended to very experienced paddlers. Paddlers on the Severn Navigation require a license: see page 41.

When?

The Severn is practical to paddle year-round from as far upstream as Pool Quay, providing that the water level is not too high. Excessive water levels are much more likely in winter, check the flow before paddling (see page 31). The Severn Uplands above Pool Quay will more reliably be practical to paddle during winter and spring, after recent rains have added decent (but ideally not excessive) flow. On the Severn Navigation (Stourport to Gloucester), the river is canalised to a depth of around two metres.

The angling 'close season' for the Severn is from 15th March until 15th June. Outside these months, the banks along some sections of the Severn will often be busy with anglers. There is plenty of room for all, however.

Which paddlecraft?

Canoes are open-topped craft within which one or more paddlers sit or kneel, propelling themselves with single-bladed paddles. They are also known as 'open canoes' or 'Canadian canoes'. Kayaks can have closed decks or open decks (known as 'sit-on-tops' or SOTs) but the key difference is that the paddler sits, propelling him- or herself with a two-bladed paddle. Some kayaks have seats for more than one paddler. Just to complicate and confuse

Cal Major and friends at Ironbridge. Photo | James Appleton.

things, in Britain it is normal to use the word 'canoe' to refer to both canoes and kayaks! Stand-up paddleboards (SUPs) are ubiquitous, now possibly outnumbering canoes and kayaks on the water. Their huge popularity (with a notable bias towards female participation) is partly explained by their accessibility (stand up, paddle) but also by the pure pleasure of traveling in this simple way, with an elevated viewpoint and your whole bodies' musculature actively involved, despite minimal connection to the craft. They are now commonly used for long trips and even multi-day expeditions. If shopping for a paddleboard, look for a model with a bit of length (10' 6" at least) for touring and decent deck elastics for carrying gear! Which is best for the Severn? All are great, but have their pros and cons. Canoes carry far more food and equipment, and are quicker to learn how to handle than kayaks. Kayaks are more manoeuvrable and less affected by wind, whilst paddleboards are extremely quick to learn but hard work in wind and limited in gear capacity. Paddleboards, with their fins, may struggle with descending shallow rapids and weirs.

The Severn by coracle?

"When George III visited Worcester about the end of the eighteenth century, an old fisherman named Peplow, living in Shrewsbury, made a voyage down the Severn in his coracle to see the King. He was more than eighty years of age ..."

W.G. Luscombe and L.J. Bird, *Canoeing*, 1948

Other kinds of paddlecraft are of course available. Inflatable kayaks are for example common, a hybrid of raft and kayak. They are easy to transport off the water (onto trains and so forth) but slow and susceptible to the wind.

The following books are recommended if you want to learn more about selecting and handling paddlecraft:

Canoeing, Ray Goodwin, Pesda Press, 2016, ISBN 9781906095543

Sit-on-top Kayak, Derek Hairon, Pesda Press, 2007, ISBN 9781906095024

Carrying gear

Whether you are travelling for a day or a week, your equipment will need protecting and waterproofing. Canoes can carry watertight plastic barrels, which helpfully keep large amounts of gear dry and protected from knocks. A recent innovation is waterproof 60-litre duffle bags, with a rolldown closure along the length of the bag; these are cheap and fit better in the canoe, but not 100% dry if submerged. For kayaks and paddleboards, the best option is to use small and flexible 'drybags' which are sealed by a roll-top closure. These fit beneath paddleboard elastics and down the back of most kayaks, with a little persuasion. Unless you buy very expensive designs with watertight seals (e.g. those from Watershed Drybags), drybags are still likely to leak; consider putting your kit in thick plastic bags inside the drybags. Camera equipment and other fragile, expensive equipment should ideally be protected in solid cases with padding, such as those produced by Peli Products. All these barrels and bags will, of course, result in soaking or destroyed kit if you forget to close and seal them properly.

Safety

This section is about *safety*: planning, selecting appropriate equipment and understanding hazards encountered on the Severn, to avoid getting into difficulty.

In normal summer water levels, the Severn downstream of Pool Quay is a forgiving and safe environment which is entirely suited to novices and the inexperienced, if a little common sense is applied in planning, selecting equipment and avoiding hazards. There are important caveats to this rule, however:

- A high water level exacerbates all normal hazards, making them harder to avoid and more consequential. We don't recommend recreational paddling in such conditions, for example when the Severn Navigation is at Red levels (see page 31), unless you are both very experienced and familiar with the river.

Loaded for adventure.

- The River Severn flows largely freely, being managed and maintained far less than rivers such as the Thames which have been engineered for navigation. Outside the Severn Navigation (i.e. above Stourport), unpredictable hazards can be encountered, especially tree hazards such as low branches or even blockages from fallen trees. On the Severn Uplands, these hazards are exacerbated by the narrow channels and swiftly-flowing water. Paddlers who want to learn more about the subject of safety (and rescue) are recommended to seek specialist training, or to consult *White Water Safety and Rescue* by Franco Ferrero (Pesda Press, 2006, ISBN 9780954706159).

Clothing and equipment
Flotation
Canoes or kayaks must have some form of fixed buoyancy to prevent them from sinking when waterlogged. This is usually achieved through combinations of inflatable air bags, solid foam or sealed chambers in the boat.

Entrapment hazards
Make sure that any ropes, straps or suchlike are securely stowed away and cannot form a loop or point of entrapment / snagging for a paddler's foot or hand. Paddleboarders should consider using a quick-release waist attachment for their leashes, being easier to release in the event of snagging or entrapment.

Buoyancy aids
A well fitted buoyancy aid is essential, and will make a swim much less dangerous. For the image-conscious, paddleboard buoyancy aids are available which can be worn unobtrusively around the waist and inflated by gas cylinders when needed.

On the Severn Navigation, you must wear a buoyancy aid.

Clothing
Your clothing needs to protect you from becoming hypothermic, by remaining warm when wet and by providing a shield from the wind. Wetsuits do this well, but will probably be over-warm and restrictive in summer. An ideal solution could be to wear polypropylene or fleece thermals with a cagoule on top. Legs need similar protection, and don't forget a warm hat for your head! Helmets also retain heat well, and may be a good idea for young or inexperienced paddlers. Footwear should offer protection when scrambling ashore on muddy banks. You should also carry spare dry clothing.

A well-equipped paddleboarder.

Sun protection

Waterproof sun cream and a brimmed hat will protect your skin, and save you from the prospect of having to paddle with painful, chafing sunburn the following day.

Phones

A mobile phone (packed in a waterproof case) is very useful to carry, for summoning assistance in an emergency. Mapping apps can also help you to monitor your progress down the river.

River hazards

Weirs

The Severn Navigation's five locks all bypass weirs (artificial dams holding back the water). There are two additional weirs at the end of the Severn Navigation; Llanthony Weir on the East Channel and Maisemore Weir on the West Channel. There are four more major weirs along the Severn Uplands; Felindre Mill (Section 1), above Dolwen Bridge (Section 2), Penarth Weir (Section 4) and Shrewsbury Weir (Sections 7 and 8). A further three weirs are small and inconsequential; below Cil-Cewydd and Leighton Bridges (Section 5) and Preston Boats Weir on the Middle Severn (Section 8).

The total of eleven major weirs along Britain's longest river is actually unusually low compared to other major rivers, the surprising thing being how freely the Severn flows. Nevertheless, these weirs are all highly dangerous. None are designed with paddler safety or enjoyment in mind! The greatest hazard is that the falling water loses energy by forming 'stoppers'; waves which fold back on themselves below drops, 'stopping' or even holding and drowning paddlers. Most of the Severn's weirs are sloping designs, with smooth faces which descend at relatively shallow angles; they can generate powerful stoppers at the base. Some of the weirs are potentially paddleable, tackled in the right conditions (in particular, very low flows) with appropriate expertise and good safety cover; however, the problem with the weirs – in particular, those on the Navigation and below – is that they are just too big in scale, and for much of the time carry too much water.

If you are not in a position of competence and experience to safely assess and paddle these potentially dangerous artificial structures, absolutely do not go near them.

If you want to learn how to assess and paddle white water safely, enrol yourself on a British Canoeing coaching scheme training course. The weirs on the Navigation have floating

Penarth Weir.

Shrewsbury Weir. Photo | Lucy Gillard.

barriers upstream of them, to deter leisure craft from wrong turns, and have signage indicating where the lock channel is. These warnings give you plenty of space to avoid the weirs and find a safe channel. On the remainder of the river there is no warning. The Canal & River Trust's byelaws prohibit descending the weirs on the Severn Navigation.

Obstacles

Be careful approaching the Severn's bridges, as the current piles onto the upstream side of the bridge pillars. Tree branches and other junk sometimes pile onto bridge pillars, causing a significant hazard. On the Middle Severn and Severn Vale, this is usually cleared fairly quickly. On the Severn Uplands, trees can remain on bridges for a long period of time and even build up into substantial blockages.

"A fallen tree with its branches in deep water running fast is what I fear most of all ... Even in a canoe these places (and they are common to all rapid rivers) where fast water sets into the bank and has eaten it out so that the rapid is on a very concave curve, want careful going. And where there are overhanging, or out-thrust, trees or branches they can be very awkward."

William Bliss,
The Heart of England by Waterway, 1933

Tree branches and bushes lurk in the water along the riverbanks. Usually these 'strainers' are simple to avoid, however rivers flow towards the outside of bends, and erode back the banks. In high water, you can find yourself being drawn towards or beneath overhanging foliage – steer to avoid. These hazards are a characteristic feature of the Severn Uplands, where low branches, overgrown bushes and

Tree blockage before Leighton Bridge.

even whole trees obstruct or completely block narrow points of the river; totally avoid blockages by portaging if necessary.

Moored boats, buoys and other fixed floating objects, most commonly encountered along the Severn Navigation, can be dangerous in high water. The current flows swiftly towards and under these things, with no cushion wave to push paddlers to safety – avoid!

Wind

Wind is a factor to consider in the open and exposed reaches of the Severn, where the banks open out. In particular, a forecast of strong south or south-westerly winds may make you adjust any paddling plans along the Severn Vale; these conditions make paddlecraft difficult to steer, or even unmanageable.

Other river users

The Severn Navigation

Powered leisure craft, up to 27.4m in length, share the water with you on the 68km Severn Navigation, between Stourport and Gloucester. Larger commercial vessels, such as gravel barges, may be encountered below Worcester. Traffic is light and infrequent; those familiar with waterways such as the River Thames will find the Severn to be practically empty by comparison. There is plenty of space for all, nevertheless remain alert when vessels do pass. Although the speed limit on the Severn Navigation is relatively high (see below), vessels passing paddlecraft are expected to keep a safe distance and reduce speed; *"Make sure that your bow wave and wash are not a hazard to other vessels"* Canal

Traffic below Holt Fleet.

& River Trust River Severn Navigation Users Guide. Move aside and give way to passing vessels; if they are concerned, they will give a single prolonged blast on their horn.

General rules of the river to be followed on the Severn Navigation:

- Keep to the right.
- Passing approaching boats, keep right and pass portside-to-portside.
- The speed limit is 6 mph heading upstream and 8 mph heading downstream.
- Vessels heading downstream (towards Gloucester) generally have right of way over those travelling upstream.

Anglers

An additional issue to consider is anglers, between 15th June and 15th March. Avoid entanglement in lines by keeping a careful eye out ahead. Paddle wide around their lines and, obviously, pass quietly and considerately.

Rowers

Rowing boats are found training at towns from Shrewsbury to Upton-upon-Severn. Rowing eights travel at up to 15 knots / 28 kph, have their backs to you, and are pointy at the ends. Obviously, keep well clear of their path. If there is a risk of collision, shout out a warning or blow a whistle.

Seeking help

If you find yourself in serious difficulty and in need of assistance, do not hesitate to call the UK emergency phone number; 999. Give details of your group, your difficulty and perhaps most importantly; your location. The operator will summon the Police, Ambulance, Fire Service, Lowland Rescue or SARA, as appropriate.

The Canal & River Trust have an emergency helpline for reporting environmental contamination, or incidents where lives or property are imminently at risk; 0800 47 999 47. In addition, there is an Environment Agency Hotline to report damage or danger to the environment, damage to structures or water escaping; 0800 80 70 60.

SARA

The Severn Area Rescue Association are an Inshore Rescue Boat and Land Search and Rescue organisation. Their five boats and 150 personnel cover the Severn Estuary from around Clevedon right upstream past Gloucester. They have Lifeboat and Rescue Stations at Wyre Forest, Upton-upon-Severn, Tewkesbury, Gloucester and Sharpness. Further info from www.sara-rescue.org.uk.

Water levels

"Heavy rains in Wales can cause the river level to rise several feet, although this may not be felt below Shrewsbury for several days after."

Percy Blandford, *Canoeing Waters*, 1966

To ascertain the level of the Severn before setting off to paddle, you have a number of options:

- Visit the government's 'Check for Flooding' website www.check-for-flooding.service.gov.uk/river-and-sea-levelsriver-and-sea-levels and search for locations along the Severn.
- Call the Floodline on 0845 988 1188 to hear recorded information and advice (select option 1 and when prompted, dial 011131).
- Check the webcams at www.farsondigitalwatercams.com which display a number of River Severn locations from Atcham Bridge (Section 8) downstream.

The river level websites give readouts from numerous gauging stations along the Severn (extending right up to the source) and its tributaries. Looking at these graphs, you'll realise that the data needs to be handled with care. The system is set up to warn of floods, and major changes are needed in the river's flow before the graphs notably alter. The graphs show the height of the river level, not the volume of the river's flow. The graphs for the Severn Uplands are more responsive to change in the river's flow; proceed with care when there has been a recent sharp increase.

Diglis Lock river gauge.

Each lock on the Severn Navigation has a mounted vertical indicator board at the exit gates, effectively a colour-coded river level gauge:

- Water within **RED** level Do not proceed. Hazardous conditions exist.
- Water within **AMBER** level Proceed with caution. Navigation conditions likely to change.
- Water within **GREEN** level Navigation conditions normal.

Electronic boards are also being installed at the locks, to impart this information.

Locks

The locks on the Severn Navigation are all substantial in size and scale, their chambers ranging from 30m in length to 92m (the immense Upper Lode Lock). None of the locks are especially user-friendly to portage and a bit of lifting and hauling is usually involved; ropes on bows and sterns are helpful. Obviously, portaging around locks can be awkward with heavy paddlecraft; a trolley is recommended for canoes. Upper Lode Lock can't be portaged. Passing through the lock chambers is by far

Upper Lode Lock.

the easiest option, providing you arrive during working hours. You must wear a buoyancy aid and carry a whistle among your group. Lock-keepers staff all of the locks, and you pass through at their discretion. In the author's experience, they are invariably helpful and friendly. They appreciate prior notice of your arrival (especially from downstream); phone ahead to let them know when you will arrive, alternatively communicate via VHF Channel 74. On arrival, simply tell them your intentions and ask them when and how they want you to enter the lock chamber. You will be asked for details of your licence or British Canoeing membership. You will have the lock chamber to yourself, the keepers are not permitted to send you in alongside powered craft. Usually you'll be asked to hold onto the (slimy) lock grab rails or chains. Paddleboarders will be expected to kneel on their board and keep body parts inside the profile of the board. The locks are open at these times:

- November to March 0800–1600
- April, May, October 0800–1800
- June-September 0800–1900

The lock names are highlighted in bold in each river section, to help you locate them easily for quick reference. See the table below for page numbers.

Expeditions

"Of the three rivers, Severn, Wye and Rheidol, that rise on Plynlimon, the Severn takes the most circuitous route to the sea, and by reason of its length and gradual fall from as high up as Newtown gives a canoe run of exceptional duration without anything serious in the way of difficulties."

British Canoe Union, *Guide to the Waterways of the British Isles*, 1935

No	Lock	Grid reference	Distance from previous lock	Distance from the source of the Severn	Telephone number	Page number
1	Lincomb Lock	SO 821 693	0km	218.1km	01299 822887	135
2	Holt Fleet Lock	SO 821 634	6.8km	224.9km	01905 620218	136
3	Bevere Lock	SO 836 594	5.7km	230.6km	01905 640275	145
4	Diglis Lock	SO 847 533	6.8km	237.4km	01905 354280	148
5	Upper Lode Lock	SP 881 329	26km	263.4km	01684 293138	156

This book's guides to sections of the Severn are of course paddling trip itineraries, each lasting from half a day to a day. Combining multiple sections to tackle a multi-day paddle down the Severn is highly recommended, offering some great challenges and experiences. There are endless possibilities for overnight or short mini-adventures, or you might consider tackling the entire length of Britain's longest river!

White-water expeditions

The Severn Uplands, especially above Pool Quay, offer good potential for multi-day white-water expeditions, but these are most likely to be practical in the wetter and colder months when camping is less comfortable and there are few public campsite options! In addition, you'd need to be flexible in your plans, starting out when the water level is healthy but not dangerously high. A journey from Llanidloes (or higher) to Shrewsbury, or even to Ironbridge / Bewdley, would pass through some beautiful wild countryside, maintaining challenge with hundreds of rapids and riffles to negotiate.

Pool Quay to the sea

This classic expedition covers the historic navigation on the Severn, with reliable water flows and reduced hazard from trees (compared to above Pool Quay). Elements of this journey are regularly used for Duke of Edinburgh's Award expeditions and suchlike. Outlined below is a fairly challenging itinerary which would complete the distance in a week, but which would require a head-down paddling approach and leave little time for exploration and tourism. The daily distances are inconsistent, but reflect the campsites available (book well ahead!).

Continuing an extra day further downstream, past Gloucester on the tidal reach to

Day	From	To	Campsite	Distance	Distance from source
1	Pool Quay	Llandrinio Bridge	The Boat House Farm	14.6km	95km
2	Llandrinio Bridge	Montford Bridge	Wingfield Caravan Park	21.5km	116.5km
3	Montford Bridge	Wroxeter	Ismore Coppice Wild Campground	37.2km	153.7km
4	Wroxeter	Hampton Loade	The Unicorn Inn & Campsite	42.4km	196.1km
5	Hampton Loade	Holt Fleet	Holt Fleet Farm Camping and Caravanning	29km	225.1km
6	Holt Fleet	Tewkesbury	Lower Lode Inn	39.5km	264.6km
7	Tewkesbury	Gloucester / Maisemore		19km	283.6km

Source to Sea by Lotte and Peter Johns

We realised quite early in 2021 that a holiday abroad was not really going to be an option (some random pandemic got in the way) so we treated ourselves to a new toy in the form of a canoe. Luckily, we didn't have to look far before we found an adventure just challenging, different and crazy enough to be irresistible; to paddle the entire length of the River Severn. Having grown up within walking distance from the source of the Severn, this seemed to be the natural starting point for our journey. However, those who have been to the source will know that it is nothing more than a large bog. A bog at the top of a big hill. Realistically, it made no sense to start at a point where the most we could achieve was a symbolic float in a muddy puddle. Nevertheless, we couldn't fall at the first hurdle and so, in the spirit of full commitment, we decided that we should carry the canoe up the mountain to the source and then all the way back down again to a point where the river was large enough for us to float! We decided that we would need some extra muscle to help us with this stage and so employed the help of our friend Zac. His response to our proposal was, *"You're idiots ... but that sounds fun!"*

After hauling the boat up on a borrowed trolley to a point where this was no longer possible, we took turns in carrying it on our shoulders; at this point we were extremely grateful for the deep dish yoke! Having made it to the top, we then had to retrace our steps back to the carpark. We donned wetsuits and continued on wheels and feet until we had passed Severn-Break-its-Neck

The source. Photo | Lotte and Peter Johns.

Newnham or Sharpness would make an excellent adventure. However, it would involve a completely different order of commitment and challenge, requiring experience and competence in the tidal environment, coupled with manageable neap tides. Paddling even further to the Severn's end below the Second Severn Crossing is feasible; see *South West Sea Kayaking* by Mark Rainsley.

Duke of Edinburgh's Award expeditions
The Duke of Edinburgh's Awards for 14–24 year olds are intended to, *'inspire, guide and support young people in their self-development'*. A key component of the awards is, *'To inspire young people to develop initiative and a spirit of adventure and discovery, by planning, training for and completing an adventurous self-sufficient journey, as part of a team'*.

Waterfall and found a point where we were able to access the river again. From here, we gorge walked with a canoe into Llanidloes ... something we have no intention of repeating! This took way longer than we were expecting and the bedrock was like sheet ice underfoot, making things particularly interesting. It was also not deep enough to float the canoe for much of the way, so it did take a bit of a battering! The large weir just upstream of the town also hindered progress significantly and we were losing light by this point. The end of a tough day was celebrated with copious amounts of chocolate when we arrived in Llanidloes.

From Llanidloes we were able to load the boat with full expedition kit and line it as we walked downriver; it was mostly deep enough for it to float, provided we weren't in it! Reaching Newtown, again, took longer than expected (there's a theme here!) but gradually the sections where we were able to paddle grew longer. There were lots of strainers and other obstacles which, while annoying at times, provided added challenge and interest as we calculated how to pass them.

Newtown to Pool Quay (day 3) continued in similar vein but we were able to paddle much more. However, the strainers we encountered were bigger; one was over 100m long! From Pool Quay (where most people start) paddling was significantly easier and we barely had to get our feet wet.

The whole trip took eight days, but for us those first three days were by far the most enjoyable as it really felt like we were on a proper adventure.

Gorge walking to Llanidloes.

Photo | Lotte and Peter Johns.

The Severn sees use by DofE expedition groups for expedition training or for final qualifying expeditions. The river suits this for a range of reasons; it flows through areas respectively fitting the DofE's definitions of 'rural' and 'wild', there is an undisputed right of navigation from Pool Quay downstream, riverside campsites are available at intervals, equipment and guides / instructors are available to hire and it is easy for a DofE Supervisor to monitor a group's progress from bridges, locks and footpaths such as the Severn Way.

The Severn has excellent potential for selecting engaging and challenging expedition aims; the wildlife and environment are easy to access and observe, whilst the region's history and culture offer more ideas; why not investigate

DofE requirements for 'canoeing and rowing' expeditions

Award	Recommended environment	Duration of expedition	Advised distances
Bronze	Canals, rivers or other inland waterways and lakes. The water and area may be familiar to participants.	2 days, 1 night, 6 hrs of planned activity daily	16–20km daily, 32–40km total
Silver	Canals, rivers or other inland waterways and lakes in rural areas. The water must be unfamiliar to the participants and present an appropriate challenge. There is an expectation that the conditions will be related to the age and experience of the participants and represent a progression between Bronze and Gold.	3 days, 2 nights, 7 hrs of planned activity daily	22km daily, 65km total
Gold	Rivers or other inland waterways and lakes in rural areas, sheltered coastal waters or estuaries. The water must be unfamiliar to the participants and must present an appropriate challenge. At Gold level routes should be in or pass through wild country. Moving water, either by current or tide, or large bodies of water, should be sought where possible.	4 days, 3 nights, 8 hrs of planned activity daily	32km daily, 128km total

Jenna's DofE expedition groups

"The Severn offers plenty of options for Duke of Edinburgh expeditions at all levels, with some great options for camping that are a bit more 'off grid' than some riverside sites. Over the years, we have used stretches of the river for Gold and Silver expedition practices, as well as qualifying expeditions, There is plenty to be found for Bronze groups too. The Severn's slow-moving nature enables plenty of independence for the groups, but there's still the option for a little excitement: the Pool Quay section gives plenty of tree hazards to dodge, Shrewsbury Weir helps with practising portages, and Jackfield Rapids offer a taste of adventure for those seeking it! Lower down the river, the weirs and locks slow things down, making it perfect for groups that prefer a gentle time ... although it could be argued that the pleasure boats offer more of a hazard than the river does! "

Jenna Sanders, DofE expedition provider
Flying Gecko Outdoors,
www.flygeckooutdoors.co.uk

the industrial heritage of Ironbridge and the Middle Severn, or the frequency of litter in the river below different settlements, for example? Further advice on DofE expeditions over water can also be found in Chapter 13 of the *Expedition Guide*:

The Duke of Edinburgh's Award Expedition Guide, Alex Davies, The Award Scheme Ltd., 2019, ISBN 978 0 905425 20 7

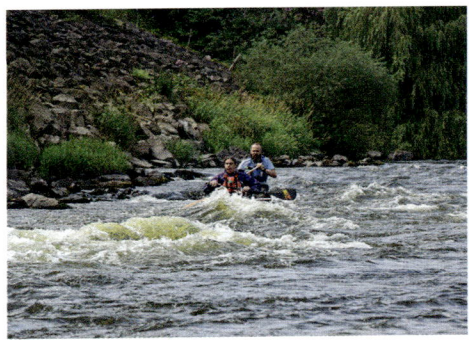
Jackfield Rapids, grade 3.

Which bank?

Throughout this book, the terms 'river left' and 'river right' are commonly used to locate features. 'River left' is simply the left-hand bank when you are looking downstream, and 'river right' is ... okay, you get it.

River left ... and river right.

Grading white water

The largely free-flowing nature of the River Severn means that there are a great number of white-water rapids along the Severn Uplands and Middle Severn. When these rapids are notable, they are graded in the text, according to the International Grading System;

Grade 1 – Moving water, unobstructed and without technical difficulties. There may be small waves and riffles to wobble the boat.

Grade 2 – Waves, small stoppers and other minor obstructions which are simple to avoid. Eddies and cushion waves may be strong.

Grade 3 – Distinctive waves, stoppers and technical difficulties. There may be drops and other powerful constrictions. The main distinguishing feature of grade 3 is that the paddler will have to follow a distinct route to avoid obstacles and hazards.

Grade 4 – Severe waves, drops, stoppers and other obstructions. The route is not easily recognisable and will usually require careful inspection from the boat or bank.

The scale goes up to grade 6! The Severn's only grade 4 white water is found in the short and little-paddled part of Section 1 above Geufron; the remainder of Section 1 is grade 3. There are plenty of grade 3 rapids along Section 2, downstream of which only Jackfield Rapids (Section 9) reaches this grade. Sections 3 and 4 have numerous grade 2 rapids, and another appears far downstream at Folly Point in Section 10. The overwhelming majority

Folly Point Rapids, grade 2.

of the rapids on the Severn are grade 1; where rapids and riffles are mentioned in the text without a grade, assume that they are grade 1. Incidentally, although high water levels increase the overall danger to paddlers, they also have the tendency to 'wash out' rapids by covering and smoothing over features. In other words, many of the Severn's rapids become easier, although not safer, in high water.

The Severn Way

The Severn Way is a 360km waymarked long-distance trail which leads from the Severn's source on Plynlimon to its end at Severn Beach in Gloucestershire, and then inland

Severn playspots

The Severn offers fairly poor value for white-water playboating. All the same, a number of spots are utilised for play by white-water paddlers.

- The 'Severn Bridge' rapid in Newtown (Section 3) forms a decent surf wave in high water conditions.
- Shrewsbury Weir (Sections 7 and 8) forms a breaking surf wave in flood conditions. Impressive and for experts only!
- Jackfield Rapids (Section 9) is the best spot on the river for basic white-water practice, with some very small features to play on.
- Folly Point Rapids (Section 10) have some very small features which are well suited to beginners.
- Maisemore Weir (Section 14) at certain levels forms a surf wave which has been played on occasion. Approach with extreme caution.
- There is, of course, also the Severn Bore (see page 181).

Severn Way signage.

Shrewsbury Weir. Photo | Cheryl Wiles.

following the Bristol Avon to Bristol. Most stretches adhere closely to the course of the river and could be used effectively as a 'walking shuttle'. The route is shown on Ordnance Survey maps and is waymarked clearly by a sailing trow symbol.

A detailed outline is available from the Long Distance Walkers Association's website www.ldwa.org.uk. The route is described in a detailed guidebook:

Walking the Severn Way, Terry Marsh, Cicerone Press, 2019, ISBN 9781786310194

Maps

The maps in this book are more than adequate to find your way along the River Severn. Ordnance Survey maps offer additional detail; the table below lists which OS maps cover each section of the river. Waterway Routes sell high quality maps of the Severn Navigation showing lock and other features, which can be used on phones and other devices. The maps are downloadable from their website www.waterwayroutes.co.uk.

Section	1:50000 Landranger map(s)	1:25000 Explorer map(s)
Source	136	214
1	136	214
2	136	214
3	136	214
4	136	214, 215, 216
5	126	216, 240
6	126	240, 241
7	126	241
8	126, 127	241, 242
9	127, 138	242, 218
10	138	218
11	138	218, 214
12	138	214, 190
13	138	190
14	138, 162	190, 179
15	162	179, OL4

Enjoying the Severn below Llandinam.

Access to the Severn

"When going on water accessible to other craft, rights are usually clearly defined ... When going on other water the canoeist is more of an explorer ..."

Percy Blandford, *Canoeing Waters*, 1966

Your right to access the majority of the River Severn is legally enshrined. Respectful and unobtrusive paddlers have encountered few problems along the sections where your right to paddle is not legally enshrined.

Pool Quay to the sea

The Severn from Pool Quay (Section 6) on the Severn Uplands downstream to the tidal waters below Gloucester is subject to an undisputed Public Right of Navigation (PRN). This exists on account of the historical use of the river for navigation as far upstream as Pool Quay.

What this means, simply, is that you can paddle freely year-round, and that **your basic right to enjoy your river heritage is legally enshrined**. Note however, that this does not give you right of access to the riverbank except for at sites with public access. If you wish to land or launch at a site, or to camp or picnic, you must first have permission from the landowner.

Stourport to Gloucester – The Severn Navigation

Large vessels can no longer reach Pool Quay and the modern-day Severn Navigation starts from Gladder Brook, just upstream of Stourport-upon-Severn. The Severn Navigation is managed by the Canal & River Trust. There are no restrictions on paddling the Severn Navigation other than the need to acquire a license:

- Licenses can be obtained online from the Canal & River Trust. This approach only makes sense if you need a license for a limited or one-off period.
- Paddlers who join British Canoeing (formerly known as the British Canoe Union) or Canoe Wales don't need to buy a license. Membership includes a license for the Severn. Simple.

The five locks on the Severn Navigation are staffed; at these locations you will be asked to show your license or British Canoeing / Canoe Wales membership card.

Gloucester to the sea

On the tidal waters from Gloucester to the Severn estuary, there is a PRN, regulated by the Gloucester Harbour Trustees. The Gloucester and Sharpness Canal is however regulated by the Canal & River Trust, so a license is required (see above).

Above Pool Quay

The right to enjoy your river heritage on the Severn upstream of Pool Quay is disputed by some. However, this certainly does not mean that doing so is illegal.

> *"Some individuals are keen to point out that 'The Law' states there is no public right of navigation on water in England and Wales. In fact, there is no statute, overriding or apparent, which supports this assertion."*
> Waters of Wales, www.watersofwales.org

The Severn above Pool Quay is refreshingly free of the farcical and legally invalid 'No Canoeing' signs which plague some rivers. The author and friends have encountered only friendly folk along these sections and have encountered no attempts to deter access. Naturally, this will only remain the case if paddlers continue to exercise discretion and politeness, coupled with absolute respect for the riverine environment.

> *"British Canoeing believes, based on a wealth of historical evidence, that there is, under common law, a public right of navigation on all rivers which are physically capable of being navigated. It is acknowledged that this position is firmly rejected by others."*
> British Canoeing, Access and Environment Charter

Use your own discretion and common sense in deciding how best to enjoy your river heritage.

Responsibilities

It should go without saying that your basic right to enjoy your river heritage comes with responsibilities; most importantly, to respect and preserve the river environment for its own sake, and for others to enjoy. The passage of paddlecraft *by definition* has minimal impact upon the riverine environment, but employ common sense to ensure that this always and absolutely remains the case. Be prepared to pick up and remove other people's waste, when you encounter it; angling and agricultural detritus is sadly not uncommon.

Enjoying the river below Newtown.

British Canoeing supply some common-sense advice in their *Paddlers' Code* and also their leaflet *You, your canoe and the environment*, downloadable from their website. Canoe Wales also publish a *Canoeing Code*.

Further information

www.britishcanoeing.org.uk – British Canoeing
www.canoewales.com – Canoe Wales
www.canalrivertrust.org.uk – The Canal & River Trust
www.gloucesterharbourtrustees.org.uk – Gloucester Harbour Trustees
www.watersofwales.org – Access to Welsh rivers
www.riveraccessforall.co.uk – Access to British Rivers

In the unlikely event that you are challenged whilst paddling the Severn, be polite and respectful, but do not be dissuaded from enjoying your river heritage. Should you find your path physically barred by individuals or if you feel threatened, report this to the police just as you would in any other part of life. Also, log any incidents with Canoe Wales or British Canoeing, who have forms for such purposes on their websites.

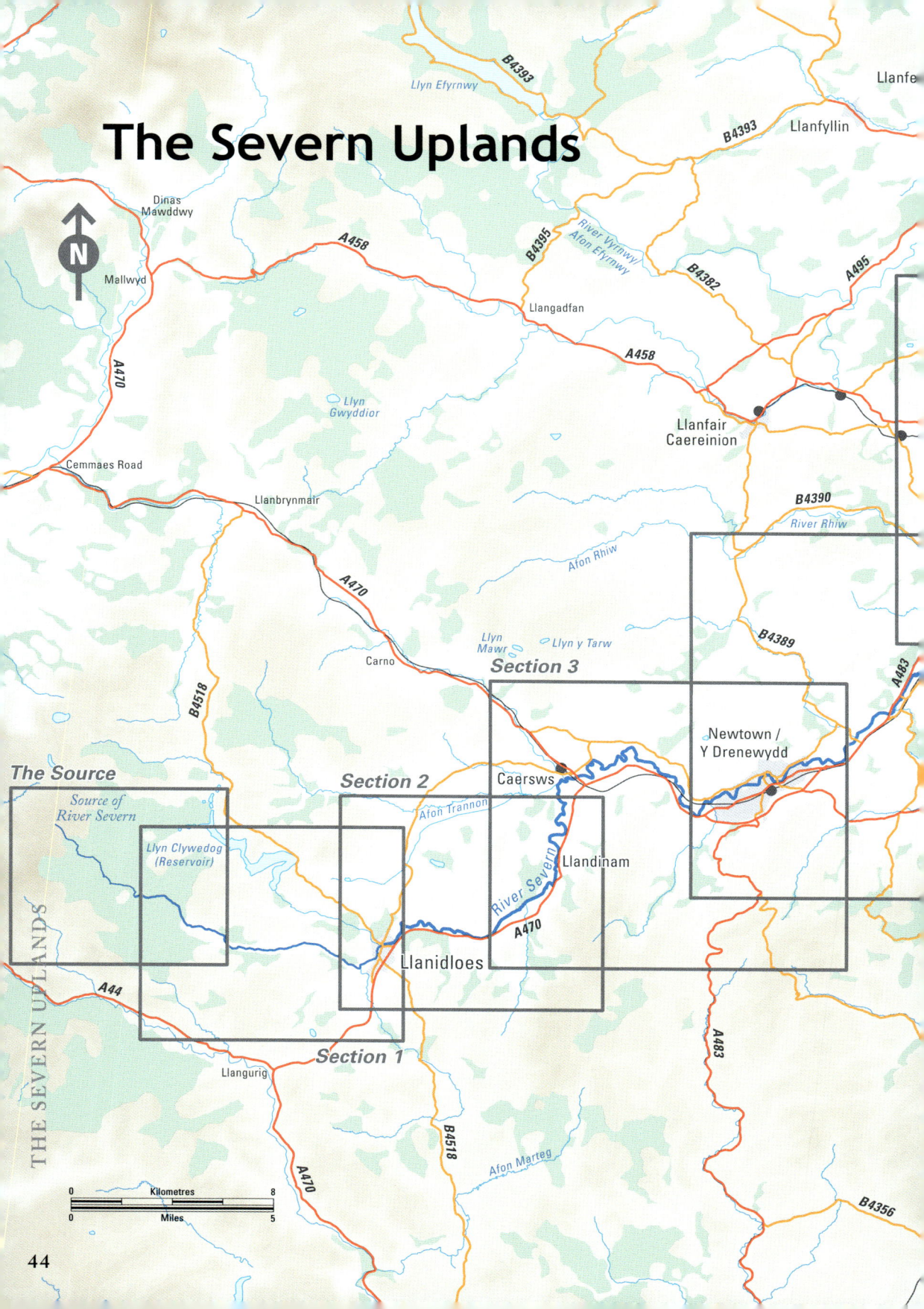

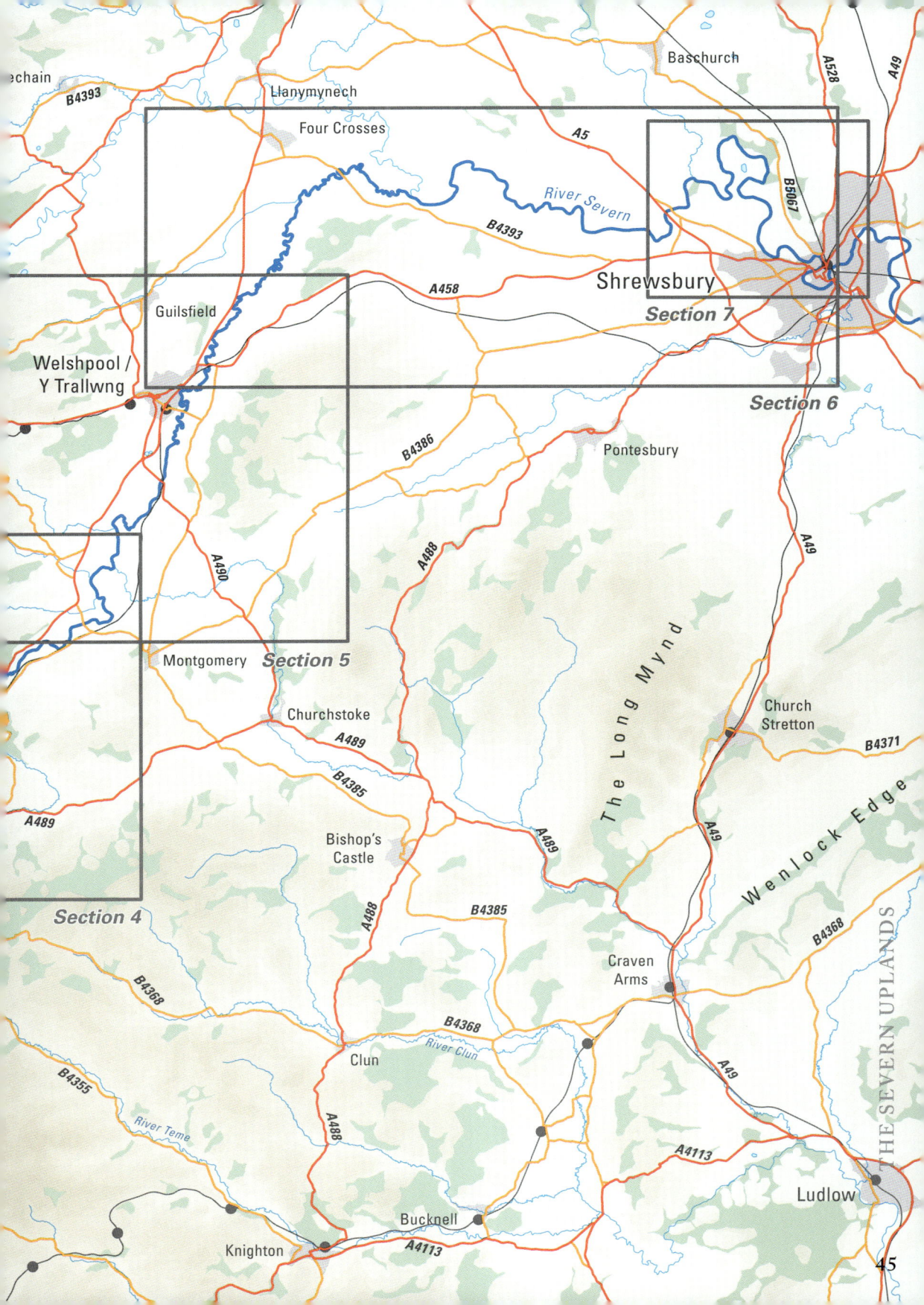

The source.

The infant River Severn.

The Source

The Source

Distance	12.8km walk, along 5.4km of the Severn
Start	△ Rhyd-y-benwch car park, Hafren Forest SN 857 869 / SY18 6PT
Finish	○ Rhyd-y-benwch car park, Hafren Forest SN 857 869 / SY18 6PT

Introduction

"Severn is born of the sodden mosses
Where smooth Plynlimon's dome is bowed
Under the rain the West Wind tosses
From tattered fleeces of sea-born cloud"

Francis Brett Young, *The Island*, 1944

The source of Britain's longest river is located at a remote spot in the Cambrian Mountains. It can however be reached relatively easily, via an engaging and accessible hill walk.

Waypoints

The source of the River Severn SN 822 899
Rhaeadr Blaenhafren SN 836 884
Rhyd-y-benwch car park, Hafren Forest SN 857 869 / SY18 6PT
Severn-Break-its-Neck Waterfall SN 863 867 / SY18 6PT

Description

The River Severn's 352 kilometres commence at a bog on Plynlimon (Welsh: *Pumlumon Fawr*, 'great five peaks'), the highest mountain in Mid-Wales. The source can be visited via an extremely well-groomed permissive path following the Severn Way from Rhyd-y-benwch car park. The route ascends through the 2,842-hectare Hafren Forest, first planted in the 1930s.

47

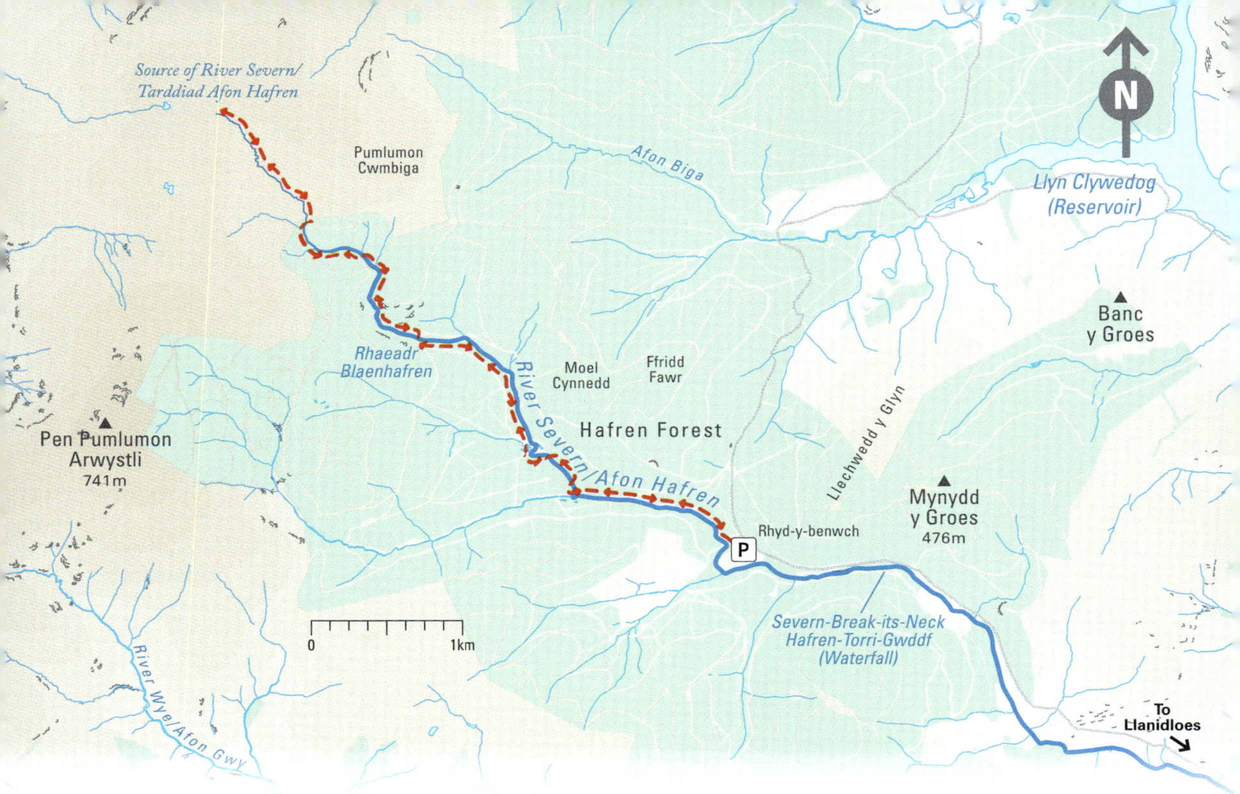

A detailed description is unnecessary as the path is so well-signposted, just a few highlights are summarised here. The route starts by following the infant Severn along boardwalks installed to protect the mosses below. Along the route it winds past several flume stations; the flows of the Severn's headwaters have been monitored for forty years. Rhaeadr Blaenhafren (*Blaenhafren*: front of Severn) is a slender waterfall encountered when a forestry track is crossed; nearby are the ruins of Hafren farm, last occupied in 1934. The path then follows the Severn up a deep gorge before emerging above the trees, with glorious views down the valley. Another forestry track is crossed and the path follows the now-tiny Severn across sphagnum moss bogs, described by Reverend J. Freeman in 1826 as, *"a long and continuous bed of boggy vegetable earth"*. In due course a large wooden post is reached, mounted on flagstones; the source! The source post is 610 metres above sea level, carved with the words *'Source of the Severn / Tarddiad Afon Hafren'*. It's a splendidly evocative

The boardwalk near Rhyd-y-Benwch car park.

spot, surrounded by pools of peaty water whose inevitable destiny is to flow beneath the Severn bridges. It is worth following the path 400m further past the source, crossing a fence to a cairn and boundary stone (SN 800 868) marked 'WWW 1865' (Sir Watkin Williams-Wynn, apparently, whose estate this was). George Borrow also came here, for the views:

"A mountain wilderness extended on every side, a waste of russet–coloured hills, with here and there a black, craggy summit ... the scene would have been cheerless in the extreme had not a bright sun lighted up the landscape."

Wild Wales, 1862

The marked path follows a different route back to the car park, much of it along forestry tracks; you may prefer to simply retrace your route.

Severn-Break-its-Neck Waterfall

An optional second marked path loops 2.8km downstream from Rhyd-y-benwch car park to visit Severn-Break-its-Neck Waterfall, located 6.4km from the source. The unwieldy name sounds better in Welsh: Hafren-Torri-Gwddf. The waterfall can alternatively be visited from the roadside; park at the large layby and turn-off, 600m down the valley from the car park, and walk down to a footbridge. The Severn plunges around seven metres into a congested gully. Severn-Break-its-Neck looks paddleable, and presumably has been ... but the clue is in the name. The gorge below the waterfall is stunningly beautiful, however accessing the river to paddle would be extremely difficult.

The 'WWW 1865' boundary stone.

Plynlimon's three rivers

Plynlimon is a sprawling upland area, famous as the source of the Rivers Severn, Wye and Rheidol:

*"From high Plynlimmon's shaggy side
Three streams in three directions glide ..."*

Lewis Glyn Cothi, *Plynlimmon*, fifteenth century

The shortest of the three rivers is the Rheidol (31km), which has its source at Llyn Llygad Rheidol, directly north of the 752m summit. The source of the River Wye / Afon Gwy (252km) is just over a kilometre to the east of the summit, and the source of the Severn (352km) is four kilometres north-east of it. Various legends tell of the rivers racing from the mountain to the sea in competition with one another:

"Three little rivers slept in a hole on the mountain, and one evening they all agreed to set off the next morning to seek their fortunes ... The Severn got up first ..."

Askew Roberts, *The Gossiping Guide to Wales*, 1877

Severn-Break-its-Neck Waterfall.

Below Severn-Break-its-Neck Waterfall.

Section 1

Severn-Break-its-Neck Waterfall to Llanidloes

Distance 11km / 9km
Start △ Severn-Break-its-Neck Waterfall SN 863 867 / SY18 6PT
Finish ◯ Llanidloes SN 954 847 / SY18 6HG

Introduction

The Severn's uppermost paddleable reaches do not disappoint. Hidden in this little-frequented valley is an excellent section of steep and continuous white water which expert paddlers will relish.

Launch points

Layby below Severn-Break-its-Neck Waterfall SN 868 867 / SY18 6PT – river left. Launch from a layby 500m downstream of the waterfall, where the road comes alongside the river. A huge boulder (the 'Severn Drinking Stone') can be seen uphill from the correct layby.

Geufron SN 881 855 / SY18 6PT – river right. Park in a rough layby overlooking the farm, a short distance down the road from the farm entrance. Walk 300m downhill to the bridge; follow the byway track into the farmyard, where you turn left onto a bridleway to the river.

Old Hall Bridge SN 908 845 / SY18 6PW – river right. Limited parking, roadside.

Llanidloes SN 954 847 / SY18 6HG – river left,

using steps below Long Bridge, or river right above Long Bridge into Severn Porte Park. Park on the roadside nearby.

Launching below Severn-Break-its-Neck Waterfall.

Description

For completists, the Severn is potentially paddleable for two kilometres upstream of Severn-Break-its-Neck Waterfall, however the waterfall and inaccessible gorge below it necessitate a long portage.

The section described here will only be possible after heavy and recent rain. You need enough flow to cover and pad the boulders, but avoid full spate conditions as the hazard from low branches would be excessive. The river is narrow and steep, only suited to very small groups of paddlers.

📷 *Above Geufron.*

Launching 500m downstream of the waterfall at the suggested layby accesses a 2.1km stretch of grade 4, albeit a messy one. The river falls away in a series of blind horizon lines, however the first two hundred metres is marred by awkward trees forcing at least one portage. The banks then close in and with little warning, the river plunges into a walled-in gorge. Rock formations in this entrance drop could cause a pin, paddle with care or portage on river left. The gloomy secret gorge below includes a lovely frothy rapid, enjoy! The banks then open out and lively grade 3 rapids bounce down to Geufron; this is the second bridge after the gorge.

Launching at Geufron gives an easier and much less obstructed trip of 8.9km. There is no warm-up! Right away, the river bobsleighs through continuous grade 2 and 3 rapids formed by small ledges and boulders. Nothing stands out as especially tricky; the point is that it is *all* rapids. Low branches will necessitate some ducking and weaving. By the time you pass beneath the bridleway bridge at Glynhafren, the gradient has eased off somewhat, but the rapids remain fairly constant.

📷 *Launching at Geufron.*

The next landmark is Old Hall Bridge, the first public road bridge crossing the Severn (the last is of course the five kilometre-long Second Severn Crossing!). Old Hall Bridge is a launch point offering a 5.6km trip and a gentler start than Geufron. Be careful here however, as at time of writing a fallen tree blocks the river just downstream.

The rapids are still continuous grade 2, with the occasional interlude at the easy end of grade 3. After two successive footbridges are passed beneath, the surrounding open farmland is replaced by steep craggy slopes; the Grand Canyon of the Severn! The rapids correspondingly feature bedrock reefs and ledges. When the water pools up, this is warning that you are approaching the weir at Felindre Mill. You first encounter a rope and a log bridge across the river, blocking your path. These are the grounds of an outdoor activity centre, closed at time of writing. Hop ashore on river left and portage discreetly along a track. The weir is paddleable, but rocky and unappealing. Be alert when you launch downstream of the weir, just out of sight is a stoppery slot, leading into a lively grade 3 rapid. Felindre Bridge crosses downstream; one of several local bridges designed by Thomas Penson.

Below Felindre Bridge, the banks open out once more, the Severn widens and the Afon Dulas flows in from river right (the author has encountered this little stream flooded and increasing the volume five-fold!). Take extreme care here, as directly downstream of the confluence, at least two strands of barbed wire stretch across the river's flow; easily the

Above Old Hall Bridge.

Bridgend Flannel Mill in Llanidloes.

most dangerous thing you will encounter all day. If in any doubt, portage along the length of the field on river right.

Your entry into Llanidloes is quite grand, with a grade 3 series of ledges on a right bend leading beneath Llanidloes Short Bridge (Thomas Penson, 1849), overlooked on river right by the tall Bridgend Flannel Mill (1834). The float through this lovely small town feels like a victory lap, below high balconies. The confluence of the Afon Clywedog on river left (dam released, flowing from Llyn Clywedog) is overlooked by the squat fourteenth century square tower of St Idloes Church on river right. Directly below are the three arches of Llanidloes Long Bridge (1826, Thomas Penson again). Land on either bank, as suits.

High flows at Bridgend Flannel Mill in Llanidloes.

Above Dolwen Bridge.

Approaching Llandinam Bridge.

Section 2

Llanidloes to Llandinam

Distance 10.5km
Start △ Llanidloes SN 954 847 / SY18 6HG
Finish ◯ Llandinam SO 025 885 / SY17 5DW

Introduction

"It is a succession of pools and little waterfalls all the way, with here and there a biggish one."

William Bliss, *Canoeing*, 1934

This short section is singled out as it offers an enjoyable dose of white-water adventure which is much less continuous than that in Section 1, and is also less reliant upon heavy rain. Those with basic white-water paddling skills can access this section, but be careful of tree and weir hazards.

Launch points

Llanidloes SN 954 847 / SY18 6HG – river left, using steps below Long Bridge, or river right above Long Bridge into Severn Porte Park. Park on the roadside nearby.

Dolwen Bridge SN 997 851 / SY18 6LX – river right, large layby beside the Riverside Café. Launch just underneath the bridge from behind the toilets, or downstream of bridge via the disused phone box.

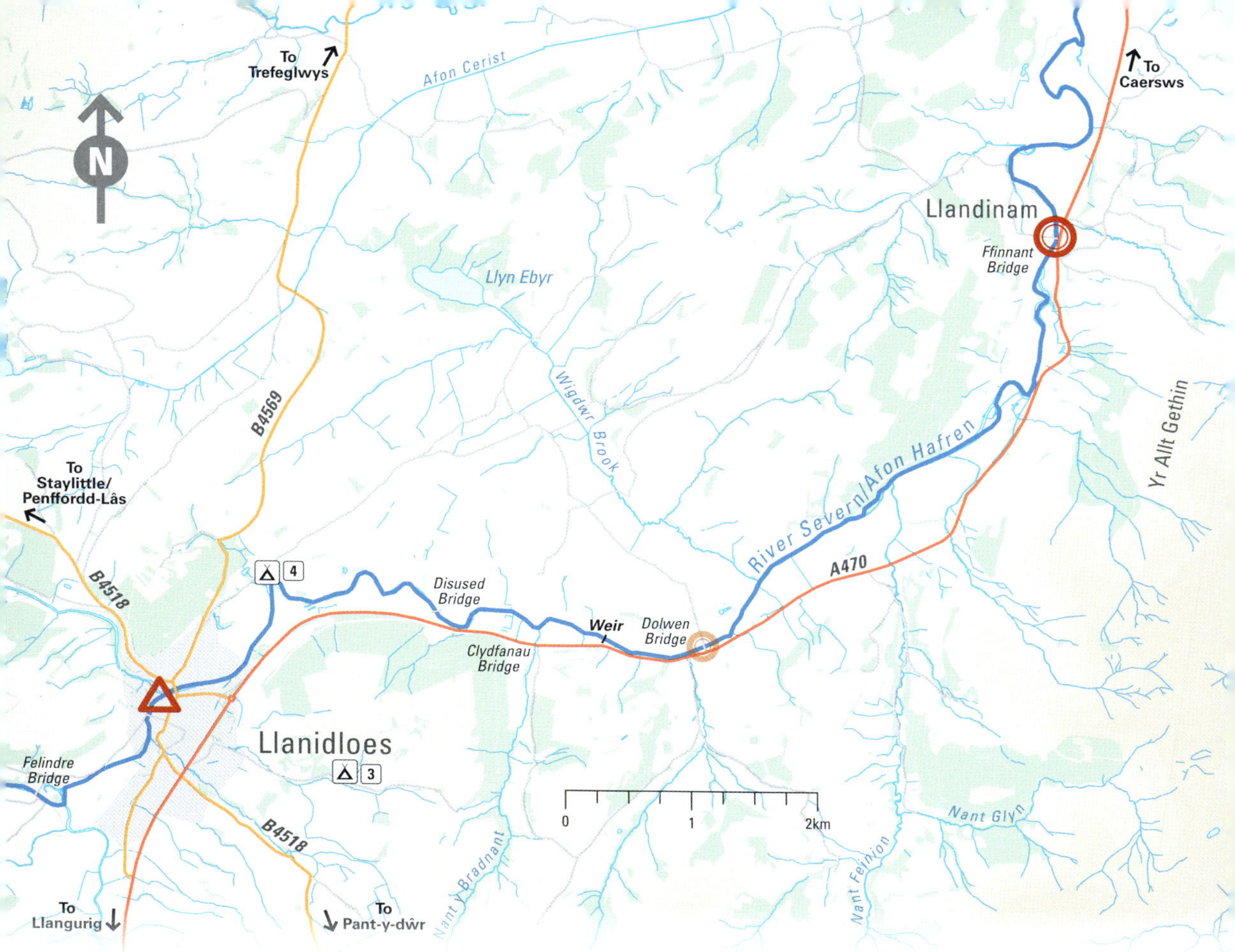

Llandinam Bridge SO 025 885 / SY17 5DW — pass through a picnic area to access the river downstream of the bridge on river left. Limited parking roadside, consider leaving vehicles in the car park located across the bridge and 200m upstream.

 Llanidloes Market Hall.

Description

The Severn from Llanidloes is predominantly a white-water trip! With a healthy flow from rainfall, boulders and bedrock ledges generate numerous distinct grade 2 rapids, with a number creeping into the easier end of grade 3; specifically, rapids where some careful route-finding is needed to get down unscathed.

📷 *Long Bridge, Llanidloes.*

"There are no really serious rapids, but some sufficiently exciting stretches between Llanidloes and Llandinam which are difficult and need care, and there is at least one little canyon or gorge."

William Bliss, Canoeing, 1934

At Long Bridge in Llanidloes, the river will need a decent flow, through at least two of the three arches. Very high levels will likely wash out the interesting rapids and make for an uncomfortable degree of tree hazard. The river quickly carries you out of town and there is nothing to report for the first three kilometres other than the occasional farm and ford. The first notable landmark is a disused and dilapidated railway bridge with tree debris piled upon its high pillars. From this point, the rapids increase in frequency and difficulty.

Bliss's *"little canyon or gorge"* is soon encountered; the river narrows between low bedrock sides and pinballs around boulders and bedrock which block a clear float through. It is easy enough to inspect or portage.

The next hazard is a bit surprising, as it is currently unmapped by the Ordnance Survey; a substantial modern weir. You won't miss it,

📷 *Disused rail bridge below Llanidloes.*

as two successive huge yellow signs along the river right bank warn you of your imminent doom, and a third one indicates where you can egress. The weir has three walled-in sloping channels and is paddleable in low flows. If at all unsure, portage on river right.

Before Dolwen Bridge, two more distinct rapids probably stretch beyond grade 2, with constricted channels and slots to negotiate. Past the bridge, at least two more rapids are relatively long and complex in scale, with extended reefs forming multiple channels and small drops; however, these are messily strewn with tree debris and your route down will be dictated by these hazards.

The white water comes to an end as the gradient eases and the river widens around islands and through a series of convoluted braids.

The weir before Dolwen Bridge.

You'll still need your white-water skills as the braids often wind tightly past or between hazardous tree debris or overhanging branches; all are avoidable with care.

The river opens out in the approach to Llandinam Bridge. There are tremendous views of the rough bracken-covered mountains narrowly hemming in the Severn from both sides.

Above Dolwen Bridge.

Yr Allt Gethin (450m) rises over 300m above the river, close on river right.

Llandinam Bridge was opened in 1846, the first iron bridge in Montgomeryshire, but it is most interesting for the statue mounted at the river right end. Llandinam local, David Davies stands looking over plans, prominent from the river and the passing A470. Davies (1818-90) built the bridge (designed by Thomas Penson) and went on to open up the Rhondda coalfields and to found Barry Docks.

Approaching Llandinam Bridge.

Radical Llanidloes

Llanidloes (church of St Idloes), the first town on the Severn, grew around the cottage industry of spinning and weaving flannel (flannel derives from the Welsh *gwlan* meaning 'wool'), exported worldwide. The introduction of factories in the late eighteenth century meant that the centre of production moved downriver to Newtown. Economic hardship encouraged radical ideas, such as Christian revivalism (Methodism); beside the timber-framed Market Hall of 1612 is a stone inscribed, *'John Wesley passed through Llanidloes at least six times on his journeys through Wales, and, according to tradition he preached on this stone on three of those occasions in 1748, 1749 and 1764'.*

More dramatically, a Chartist uprising took control of the town for five days in 1839 (Chartists wanted the vote for all men). Troops regained the town and occupied it for a year, along with harsh sentencing for more than a hundred townsfolk.

Nowadays, the most radical thing in this attractive, small town is the bookshop, which comes with its own resident harpist.

Paddling through Newtown.

Caersws Bridge.

Section 3

Llandinam to Newtown

Distance	18.5km
Start	△ Llandinam SO 025 885 / SY17 5DW
Finish	◯ Newtown SO 110 916 / SY16 1AA

Introduction

"Very beautiful, wild and yet wooded enough, and romantic and remote from man."

William Bliss, *Canoeing*, 1934

The words 'beautiful', 'wild' and 'remote' are 100% appropriate. Bliss estimated this section to be nearly twice as long as it actually is, and it is easy to see how he thought this; the Severn winds endlessly through open country, undisturbed by settlements.

Launch points

Llandinam Bridge SO 025 885 / SY17 5DW – pass through a picnic area to access the river downstream of the bridge on river left. Limited parking roadside, consider leaving vehicles in the car park located across the bridge and 200m upstream.

Caersws SO 032 917 / SY17 5DX – river left. Launch on river left directly below the A470 bridge at Caersws, from Severn Street. Limited parking in the village. Alternatively, follow Severn Street 150m to a left bend where a track leads off on the right. Park and follow the track 150m to the river.

Newtown SO 110 916 / SY16 1AA – river right. Shortbridge Street car park. Steps to access the river.

Description

At Llandinam Bridge, overlooked by the statue of David Davies, the Severn is hemmed-in by trees. Shortly after the start however, the river widens; you'll need a decent current from recent rainfall to float and enjoy the shingly riffles of this section's first half. The first five kilometres to Caersws wind sedately from one side of the flood plain to the other, with open banks. The views are stunning, especially when sunshine adds colour to the surrounding hills; Moel Iart rises to 438m on river right and the Iron Age hillfort of Cefn Carnedd looks down on the valley from river left. When the river bends back upon itself, you are rewarded with grand views up the cleft of the Severn valley towards Plynlimon, into the heart of the Cambrian Mountains. This is a classic U-shaped valley, scoured out during the Devensian glaciation around 20,000 years ago.

"Past Llandinam under the ridge of Moeliart and the bluff of Cefn Nith it runs through some of the most beautiful wilds of Wales, but though here and there are long deep pools and, in the

📷 *Llandinam Bridge.*

📷 *Below Llandinam.*

spring at any rate, it carried a good body of water, there are more rapids and waterfalls than pools."

William Bliss,

The Heart of England by Waterway, 1933
Bliss might have overstated the 'waterfalls', but small riffles keep you entertained as the river scours out fresh banks on wide corners. Llandinam Hall, a huge seventeenth century farmhouse, is passed close on river right after three kilometres from Llandinam Bridge. The banks close in and a kilometre past the farmhouse, the river braids around several overgrown islets; if you select an unlucky channel, you will find your path blocked by trees and be forced to portage.

The Severn is augmented by two successive tributaries which join from river left in just 400 metres; the Afon Cerist and then the Afon Carno. These are followed by Caersws Railway Bridge and then Caersws Bridge alongside the village of Caersws, which is on river left.

Past the three low arches of Caersws Bridge (which have limited clearance in flood), the

Ancient Caersws

Quiet Caersws gives few clues to its ancient past. It is possibly *Mediomanum*, base of the Celtic Ordovices tribe who resisted the Romans from North and Mid-Wales and it may have been the site of Caractacus's ill-fated last stand, c50AD. Roman chronicler Tacitus described how, *"Such enthusiasm confounded the Roman general. The river too in his face, the rampart they had added to it, the frowning hilltops, the stern resistance and masses of fighting men everywhere apparent, daunted him."*

Caer- means fort, *-sws* possibly refers to a female leader. This became a far-flung outpost of the Roman Empire, with traces of two forts; one was built c43AD (directly following the conquest) and is located within a bend of the river, a kilometre east of the village, whilst the second dates from c70AD and is near the railway station and Afon Carno. A Roman road passes through the village and crosses the river.

Severn returns to wide ambles across the flood plain, unbothered by the outside world. A glance at the Ordnance Survey map will reveal numerous oxbow lakes littering the plain, testimony to previous amblings of the river, across eons of time. Occasional tree branches draping across the river need your attention, and five kilometres below the bridge, a portage may be required where the river sprawls, for a second time, around overgrown islands. This is directly upstream of Festival Bridge, an isolated white suspension footbridge built in 1951 by David Rowell and (presumably) named in honour of the Festival of Britain that year.

After a further three kilometres of glorious solitude, the railway crosses at Doughty Bridge and after a further two kilometres, again at Scafell Bridge. By the time you reach the second rail bridge, the river has distinctly narrowed. When Mochdre Brook joins on river right you are entering Newtown. This is the largest town in Powys, yet it remains largely unseen over the following three kilometres and only makes an appearance at the very end of this section. It is hidden from sight by a buffer zone of parkland and fields along both banks, themselves obscured behind small cliffs which now line the water's edge. Another new feature is rapids, significantly livelier than those encountered so far! A number of rapids reach grade 2 and one is particularly notable; an ominous horizon line is followed by a long, weir-like rapid, with sizeable waves and stoppers to steer through. In high water, this is a popular playspot. This is

Upstream of Long Bridge, Newtown.

📷 *Long Bridge, Newtown.*

📷 *St Mary's Church, Newtown.*

directly upstream of Dolerw Park Footbridge and we'll name it the 'Severn Bridge Rapid' as this 1973 footbridge is apparently a (reduced-size) replica of the M48 Severn Bridge, encountered 300 kilometres downstream.

Long Bridge comes into view directly after, three stone arches at the heart of Newtown. Thomas Pensen designed it in 1826 and it was widened in 1857 following a traffic accident, with cast iron walkways added. You can't see much of Newtown's centre due to high flood defences, but you will spy the timber belfry of St Mary's Church peeking over the flood wall on river right. After repeated flood damage, the church was abandoned in 1856 and lies in ruins, only the tower having been restored in 1939.

Halfpenny Footbridge is a concrete affair, built in 1972 when much of the flood defence engineering was done; it's not the first bridge to carry this name, the river has destroyed three others at this spot since 1830! The landing steps leading to Shortbridge Street car park are directly below, on river right.

Robert Owen and Newtown

Newtown / Y Drenewydd was founded by charter in 1279; this river crossing, known as Llanfair Cedewain, was seized from Llywelyn ap Gruffudd after the capture of Dolforwyn Castle.

Newtown was the birthplace of Robert Owen (1771–1858). Despite being a wealthy industrialist, Owen was a pioneering socialist. He poured his fortune into building 'model communities' for his factory workers in Lanarkshire and the US, seeking to improve their rights and living conditions. He is best known as an early advocate of trade unions and a founder of the Co-operative movement (still with us, in the form of Co-op supermarkets and banks). His grave is alongside (now ruined) St Mary's Church; it is surrounded by Art Nouveau railings decorated with the words, *'Each for All'*. There is also a statue of Owen directly across the road from the Shortbridge Street car park launch point.

Below Newtown.

Brynderwen Bridge.

Section 4

Newtown to Garthmyl

Distance 13.4km
Start ⚠ Newtown SO 110 916 / SY16 1AA
Finish ⭕ Caerhowel Bridge SO 196 981 / SY15 6RT

Introduction

"A beautiful valley, which was enriched with the Severn meadows and pastures, and bounded, on each side of the river, with moderate hills generally mantled with woods."

Henry Wyndham, *A Tour through Monmouthshire and Wales*, 1781

This short section below Newtown is effectively a white-water trip; numerous distinct, grade 2 rapids and ledges focus your attention on the river. Try and look up from time to time, because the surroundings are simply lovely.

Launch points

Newtown SO 110 916 / SY16 1AA – river right. Shortbridge Street car park. Steps to access the river.

Cil Gwrgan Bridge SO 143 933 / SY16 3AQ – small layby on river right, a public footpath leads through a gap in the hedge. Launch downstream of the bridge from beside the footpath.

Caerhowel Bridge SO 196 981 / SY15 6RT – limited roadside parking near the bridge. Steep access to the water downstream of the bridge on river right, from the public footpath.

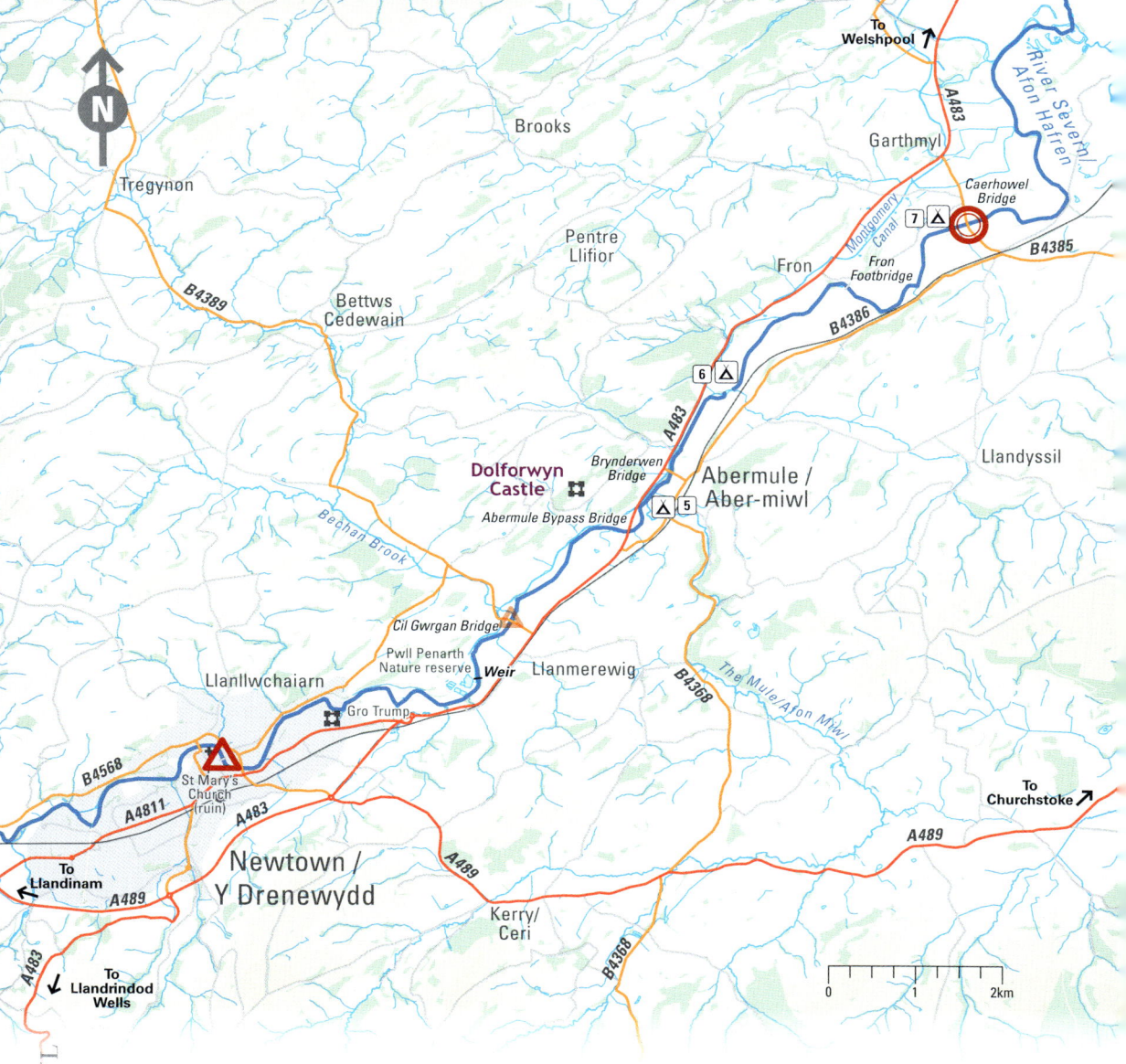

Description

The Severn is relatively narrow in Newtown, constrained by flood defence barriers. You will need enough flow to float comfortably through the town without scraping, but more is preferable as many of the rapids to come flow over wide, shallow reefs. Launching from the steps at Shortbridge car park, you are immediately into easy, unobstructed rapids bubbling over boulders and bedrock reefs. These continue past Newtown Bypass Bridge, after which the river opens out somewhat.

Departing Newtown, you encounter the first of the numerous, grade 2 rapids which pepper the river as far as Caerhowell Bridge.

Penarth Weir.

These rapids are mildly 'technical', meaning that some manoeuvring will be necessary to avoid shallow rocks or find the best channel through bedrock reefs; great fun! There are too many rapids to describe, but one you'll recognise early on is a succession of ledges at the first sharp right bend. This is overlooked on river right by Gro Tump, the earthworks of a motte-and-bailey castle.

"The Montgomeryshire Severn is a river of unexplored beauty, and comparatively few have seen where it breaks over the Penarth Weir in an eleven-foot drop."

Brian Waters, *Severn Stream*, 1949

When the rapids ease and the river pools up, the river left bank is a sewage works, followed by the reclaimed land of Pwll Penarth Nature Reserve; be on the lookout for Penarth Weir. More pertinently, be on the lookout for the beach upstream of the weir on river left, where you'll take out to portage. A track leads around to a launch point downstream of the weir. Penarth Weir is a curved sloping bowl, followed by several smaller ledges; it is paddleable in very low flows but forms a lethal stopper in higher levels. This massive construction fifty kilometres from the source, is the largest artificial obstruction on the river so far. There is nothing comparable until Shrewsbury Weir and then the start of the Navigation (50 and 160 kilometres downstream, respectively). The weir was built, originally in timber, to feed the 53km Montgomery Canal. It currently marks the canal's western terminus, but five further locks previously extended to Newtown Basin.

Cil Gwrgan Bridge.

Above Caerhowell Bridge.

Cil Gwrgan Bridge at Aberbechan is recognisable by its three, wide, brick spans, built in 1862. A complex series of shallow ledges and stoppers lead down to the bridge:

"I got out and surveyed it from the bridge above. It was certainly rocky, very rapid, and it looked bad."

Geoffrey Boumphrey, *Down River*, 1936

Assuming that you survive Cil Gwrgan Bridge rapid, plenty more follow downstream as the river winds beneath wooded hills.

"This part of Wales seems extraordinarily rich in prehistoric or barely historic remains. Almost every hill has its camp or castle tump."

Geoffrey Boumphrey, *Down River*, 1936

High on river left, the ruins of Dolforwyn Castle overlook the river on its approach to (bland) Abermule Bypass Bridge (1975). Dolforwyn means 'maiden's meadow' ...

"Near here, according to local tradition, Sabrina was drowned and gave her name to the Severn. She is supposed to have fled from her father's castle on top of the precipitous hill overlooking the river, pursued by her angry stepmother."

Brian Waters, *Severn Stream*, 1949

So, the river takes its name from this spot, although specifically which spot that might be is of course obscure. See page 21 for more about the legend of Sabrina.

The confluence of The Mule on river right, a small stream indicates that you are passing Abermule village. A rapid below the confluence was described as a, *"miniature canyon"* by Geoffrey Boumphrey; although he did capsize and break his kayak here, he might have exaggerated about the canyon bit.

Brynderwen Bridge is a real treat. Those who built this (to Thomas Penson's design) clearly

Dolforwyn Castle

The castle was built by Llywelyn ap Gruffudd in 1273, asserting his Welsh overlordship acknowledged by Henry III in 1267 (at Rhydwhyman, see Section 5). However, the new king, Edward I, saw it and him as a threat and in 1277, Dolforwyn Castle was besieged and destroyed; a pretty short career for a castle! The ruins occupy a great location, if you can find time and space to trek up there; Cadw maintain the site and entrance is free.

◎ Caerhowel Bridge.

felt real pride, as they individually forged the huge letters which span the entire arch, spelling out, *'THIS SECOND IRON BRIDGE CONSTRUCTED IN THE COUNTY OF MONTGOMERY WAS ERECTED IN THE YEAR 1852'.*
The last five kilometres to Caerhowel Bridge flow away from signs of civilisation, backed by mountain views and punctuated by riffly rapids which now appear more occasionally. The only landmark is Fron Footbridge, a suspension bridge built in 1926 by David Rowell & Co.
Caerhowell Bridge (Penson again, 1858) crosses the river via two, white arches above an island; you'll want the river right arch if you are finishing here. The village of Garthmyl is 900m north of the bridge.

"We ran through some of the best country we had found so far ... Later on, when we had got down to more civilised parts, even though weirs and rapids were things of the past, we still thought regretfully of that wild stretch before Welshpool and wished we were back on it."

Geoffrey Boumphrey, *Down River*, 1936

Variations

The Montgomery Canal passes both Aberbechan Bridge and Garthmyl, making a 'canal shuttle' potentially possible. See below.

Paddling the Montgomery Canal

The Montgomery Canal was opened between 1796 and 1819, linking Newtown and the Llangollen Canal. In effect, it extended the navigable River Severn by following the river upstream from Pool Quay to Newtown Wharf. The canal was closed in 1944 following a breach, however it has been undergoing gradual restoration since the 1980s.

At present, a 19km stretch has been fully restored for powered craft; between Berriew (1.5km north of Garthmyl) through Welshpool and past Pool Quay to Arddleen. However, the unrestored stretches following the Severn further upstream as far as Aberbechan Bridge are potentially paddleable. This means that it is (in theory) possible to paddle about 22km back 'upstream' along the canal after paddling the Severn from Newtown to Pool Quay. This would make for quite the adventure; the canal is extremely attractive, much of it being an SSSI, although narrow and often overgrown. It winds through some lovely countryside but also regularly parallels the A483, from which is it easily 'inspected'.

A Canal & River Trust license is required; their website contains excellent information on launching on and paddling on the canal, including the unrestored stretches.

Weir below Leighton Bridge.

Below Buttington Bridge.

Section 5

Garthmyl to Pool Quay

Distance 20.1km
Start △ Caerhowel Bridge SO 196 981 / SY15 6RT
Finish ○ Pool Quay SJ 247 099 / SY21 9JT

Introduction

"The Severn winds its serpentine course thro' this vale, and heightens the beauties of the prospect. On each side the vale, the hills tower in majesty and grandeur ... Some even venture to affirm that it is not equalled by any in Britain."
Joseph Craddock, *Letters from Snowdon*, 1770
Craddock was viewing the Severn from Powis Castle. This is a stretch of remarkable, riverine beauty; the river spreads across the valley floor in unmanaged braids and meanders, the banks and islands strewn with natural flood detritus. At Welshpool the river counterintuitively becomes smaller, changing character to a narrow tree-lined corridor.

Launch points

Caerhowel Bridge SO 196 981 / SY15 6RT – limited roadside parking near the bridge. Steep access to the water downstream of the bridge on river right, from the public footpath.
Cil-Cewydd Bridge SJ 227 040 / SY21 8RT – launch upstream of the bridge from public

footpaths on river left or river right. Parking over 100m away along A490 in Cilcewydd.

Leighton Bridge SJ 236 069 / SY21 8FJ – river left, on B4381 east of Welshpool. Unload on side track just past Leighton Arches caravan site. Carry boats past gate and along edge of field, to launch under the bridge. Leave vehicles here or roadside in Severn Farm Enterprise Park, 600m away.

Pool Quay SJ 247 099 / SY21 9JT – river left.

📷 *Caerhowel Bridge.*

Large layby on A483, 1.5km towards Welshpool from the Powis Arms. Go through a metal gate to the river, or use the public footpath gate (Offa's Dyke Path National Trail).

Description

Those who have paddled from Pool Quay (Section 6) will be amazed by the greater width and scale of the Severn further upstream. In normal summer levels, there are shallows and wide areas of exposed gravel; to be enjoyable, the river needs to have a reasonable flow from recent rain. Judge the viability of this trip from Caerhowel Bridge; the gravel banks should be covered and it should be possible to float the rapid downstream without scraping. High water levels are best avoided as there is a significant hazard from flood debris; trees which pile up on bends and islands, and in one case block the river. Be alert, as the river flows swiftly towards these hazards.

The rapids between Caerhowel Bridge and Pool Quay are riffles and small waves, far less notable than on Section 4. The banks in the first five kilometres are often open, giving wide vistas of these mountainous borderlands. Rhydwhyman was the site of a ford at the border between Powys and Montgomeryshire, where Henry III met Llywelyn ap Gruffudd in 1267 and recognised him as Prince of Wales in the Treaty of Montgomery; a significant moment in Welsh history. The peace was short-lived; Edward I invaded in 1277 and crushed Welsh independence. The left bend below Rhydwhyman arcs around the earthworks of Forden Gaer Roman Fort, a frontier cavalry station.

Weir below Cil-Cewydd Bridges.

In the 1.5km between the confluence of the River Rhiw on river left and the Camlad on river right, the Severn spreads onto the plain in an extraordinary network of braided channels around huge, shingle islands, flanked by oxbow lakes, cut off by the river's changing course. This is the 41-hectare Dolydd Hafren nature reserve, and it gives a rare glimpse into how our rivers looked before modification and management. Two bird watching hides overlook the channels, try to minimise noise and disturbance as you pass through.

The Camlad is the only river to flow into Wales from England! From this small tributary to Cil-Cewydd Bridge, the Severn alternates between flowing wide and open, and contorting around islands via narrow channels overgrown with willow; some ducking and weaving may be necessary.

A random hazard before Cil-Cewydd Bridge, easily spotted and avoided, is a series of iron girders sticking up from the riverbed. Cil-Cewydd Bridge itself (yet another of Thomas Penson's efforts) and the railway bridge shortly after, give notice that you are approaching Welshpool, although the river skirts around the town. A small weir follows the bridges; two tiny slopes form waves which will trouble no one. Severn Caravan Park, with camping possible, is on river right.

"The river fringed with willow and ash and beech, level fields of pasture on the right rising gradually to higher ground and, a mile or two ahead, forming the south-west spires of Long Mountain; and on the left, more thickly wooded and climbing more steeply to over one thousand feet."

Geoffrey Boumphrey, *Down River*, 1936

Tree blockage before Leighton Bridge.

Powis Castle.

There are grand views on river right of 408m Long Mountain and glimpses of the distinctively steep-sided Breiddon Hills, with which paddlers continuing into Section 6 will become very familiar. Keep an eye also on the wooded ridge forming the river left horizon; eventually you'll spot the red sandstone of Powis Castle, 1.5km from the river.

The views vanish and you plunge into a narrow and endlessly winding corridor, hemmed in on all sides by high banks and trailing willows. The outside world is mostly hidden, giving few clues as to your location. This continues right past Welshpool; the Severn is seemingly embarrassed by the town! The author had an encounter hereabouts with an otter swimming right across the bow of his kayak, unhurried and seemingly unbothered; he was however the last in the group to actually notice it.

"We passed Welshpool that day, and came to a part of the river where it was heavily overhung by trees which almost met overhead. At times we might have been in the jungle ..."

Geoffrey Boumphrey, *Down River*, 1936

In low water conditions, blockages of trees

Powis Castle

The medieval castle and its terraced gardens overlooking the Severn were rebuilt and restored in the eighteenth century by the son of Robert Clive ('Clive of India'). It's well worth visiting this opulent National Trust property after paddling, to view just a fraction of the immense treasures pillaged from Bengal by Clive whilst representing the East India Company. Clive, one of our more controversial imperial heroes, is commemorated with a statue in Shrewsbury which he represented as an MP and, later, mayor.

make a number of portages necessary. With a healthy flow it should be possible to find a channel bypassing all bar one; a large island encountered shortly before Leighton Bridge has accumulated an impressive wall of wood debris, extending across all channels; it's easy enough to bypass it with a short portage into the river right channel.

Unattractive Leighton Bridge on the B4381 is the closest launch point to Welshpool. Shortly

Sand martin burrows below Welshpool.

downstream is a small weir, falling maybe 30cm vertically. This is fun to descend, but inspect for a rock-free route. Following the weir, the river delves back into the tree-tunnel, with perhaps even more convoluted winding than before, but with no blockages in recent years. The only signs of Welshpool are a few glimpses of industrial and agricultural buildings; the author rescued a sheep trapped by the steep banks and is still watching the post for his medal.

Buttington Railway Bridge and Buttington Bridge indicate that you've finally passed Welshpool; the three kilometres from Leighton Bridge took the author a full hour in summer

What to see in Welshpool

The pleasant market town of Welshpool / Trallwng was simply 'Pool' until 1835, when it was renamed to distinguish it from the English Poole! The town grew from the flannel industry and from its position on the Montgomery Canal. There are many Georgian buildings, unusually with brick facades; look for a small hexagonal building which housed a cockfighting pit. The quirky Powysland Museum, in a former warehouse alongside the canal, offers an insight into the region's history and culture. The Welshpool and Llanfair Light Railway, a two-foot gauge line serving the Banwy valley, offers a bit of steam nostalgia. After closure in 1956, enthusiasts reopened the line which now ends at the town's fringes but used to run right through Welshpool's central streets.

Above Buttington Bridge.

levels! Buttington Bridge is a graceful cast iron arch from 1872, crossed by both the A458 and Offa's Dyke Path National Trail. This spot has quite the past. It is possibly the location of the Rhyd-y-Groes ford in *The Mabinogian*, a series of ancient Celtic tales first compiled in the fourteenth century: *'a great host of King Arthur gathered on a flat island below the ford'*. In 893, the Welsh and the Mercians defeated the Danes here; 400 skulls were uncovered when a school was built in the nineteenth century, although they could have been victims of the battle fought in 1039 between English and Welsh forces. Henry Tudor forded here in 1485, en route to victory at the Battle of Bosworth.

Be careful as it is easy to miss the take-out at Pool Quay; nothing much distinguishes it other than a right bend (the third after Buttington Bridge) where you'll hear traffic nearby.

Variations

The Montgomery Canal passes both Garthmyl and Pool Quay, making a 'canal shuttle' potentially possible. See page 73.

Buttington Bridge.

📷 Montford Bridge.

Vyrnwy confluence.

Section 6

Pool Quay to Montford Bridge

Distance 36.1km
Start △ Pool Quay SJ 247 099 / SY21 9JT
Finish ⊙ Montford Bridge SJ 432 152 / SY4 1EB

Introduction

"No villages come near, no farms are seen from where you float, and only in three places all the way from Welshpool to the Vyrnwy do you catch a glimpse of any human habitation."

William Bliss, *The Heart of England by Waterway*, 1933 – describing 1889

The Severn tos and fros in a crazy series of meanders, seemingly in little hurry to arrive anywhere. Imposing Breidden Hill rears above and indeed dominates this impressively remote section.

Launch points

Pool Quay SJ 247 099 / SY21 9JT – river left. Large layby on A483, 1.5km towards Welshpool from the Powis Arms. Go through a metal gate to the river, or use the public footpath gate (Offa's Dyke Path National Trail).

Rhyd-esgyn SJ 278 148 / SY21 9LD – river left, end of Rhyd-esgyn Lane. Very limited parking, launch from public footpath between lane and river.

Llandrinio Bridge SJ 298 169 / SY22 6SG – launch on river left from public footpaths,

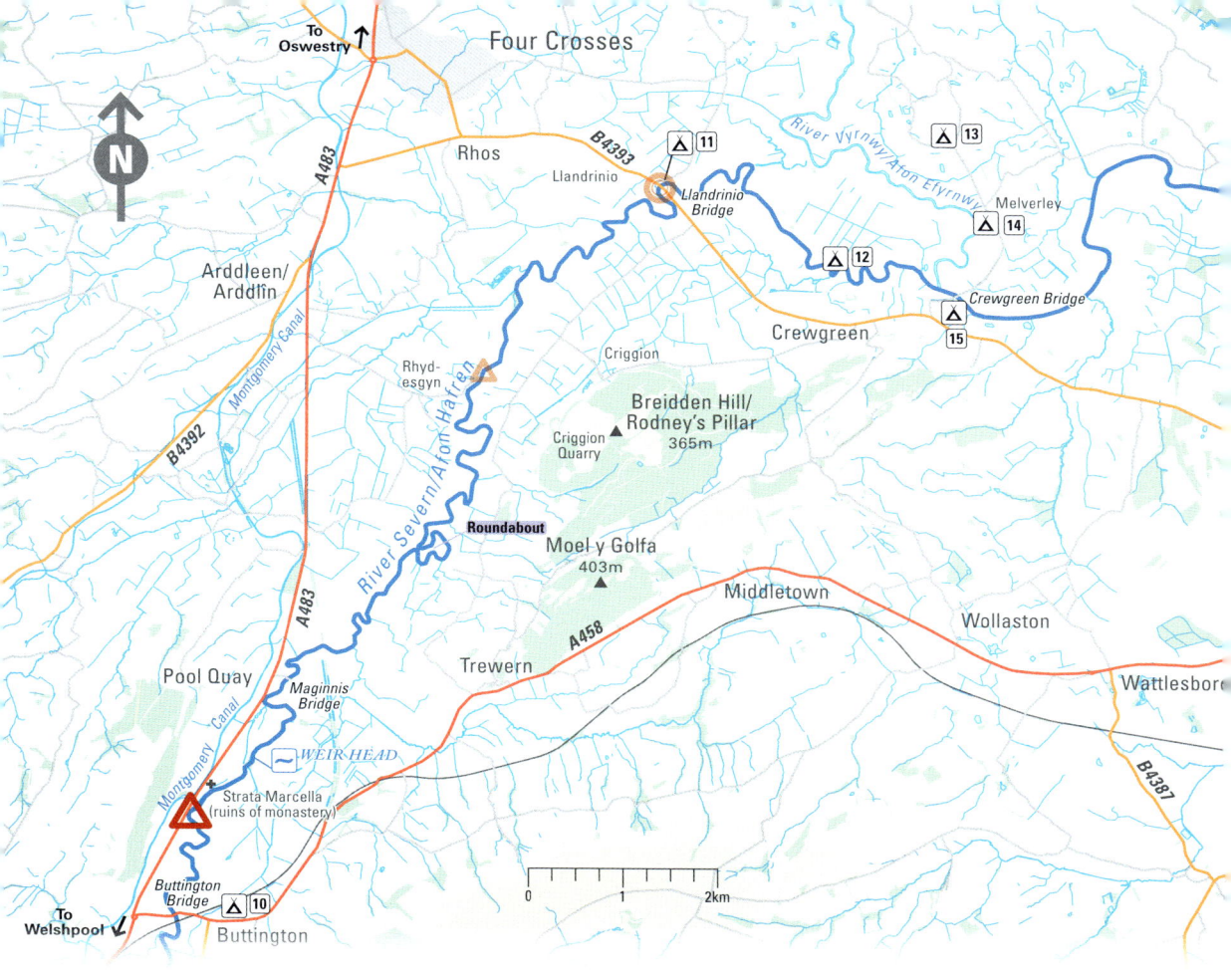

Description

upstream or downstream of the bridge (downstream is in front of the campsite). Park in a layby beside the B4393.

Crewgreen Bridge SJ 329 157 / SY5 9BS – park in roadside laybys on either side of the bridge, launch from public footpaths on either bank. River right is probably easiest.

Montford Bridge (Wingfield Caravan Park) SJ 432 152 / SY4 1EB – river right, above Montford Bridge's bridge. Parking area behind the Wingfield Arms. Only with prior arrangement and payment of a launching fee.

This section is paddleable year-round; it is more channelled and hence doesn't require a boost from rain. It can however be slow-going in low water levels and is a long day out unless you divide it into two, perhaps with a camp.

Immediately after launching, the river is engulfed by a corridor of trees and bushes. The few traces of Strata Marcella, a Cistercian Abbey founded in 1170, pass unnoticed. A rocky rapid at Weir Head marks the site of a weir and mill built by monks, marking the upward limit of the historic Navigation. The

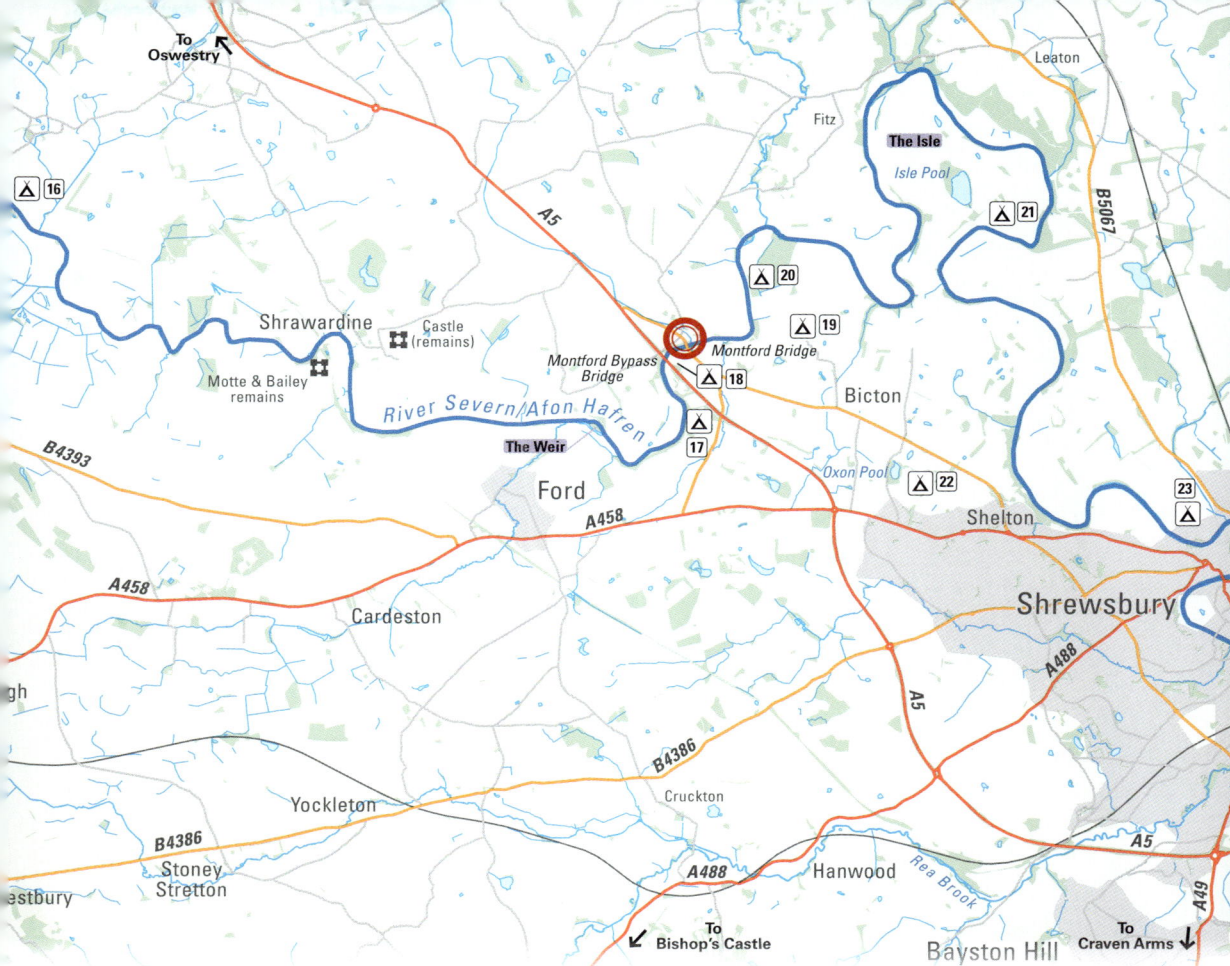

weir was destroyed by an 1881 flood.

When the river bends sharp right and you hear the road above, this is Pool Quay itself; today just a pub and timber-belfry-ed church mark the uppermost limit reached by trows (sailing barges) which had made it upriver from Gloucester and beyond. They were loaded up with goods brought down the Severn valley by canal from Newtown.

Those who have survived the jungly stretch of river past Welshpool will note that from Pool Quay, the river becomes noticeably less obstructed. The valley sides also open out as the river emerges onto a plain which extends as far as Wenlock Edge in Shropshire. Until the Severn burst through at Ironbridge Gorge, it may have been the bed of vast, ice-dammed 'Lake Lapworth'. The Severn winds tortuously, bounded by earthen flood embankments, known locally as *argae* (barrier); those as far as the River Vyrnwy confluence were engineered by Telford. One particularly crazy series of bends is called Roundabout; the river eventually doubles back within 50m of itself, at a small rapid.

You won't need a compass, because you have

Criggion Quarry on Breidden Hill.

Rodney's Pillar.

the Breidden Hills. These volcanic, basalt hills dominate the Severn through many hours of paddling, almost always remaining close to hand and in view ... yet never in the same direction. The hills line the river right side of the valley, yet are only intermittently on the river right side of the river! The first summit passed is 403m Moel y Golfa, followed by 365m Breidden Hill. The latter hill is much closer to the river, is dauntingly steep-sided and is scarred by Criggion Quarry, which has bitten a chunk from its flank. A monument known as Rodney's Pillar (no sniggering, please) is visible at the summit.

"Wherever the banks open out and the trees fall back there are the Breidden Hills high above you – to your right, to your left – in front of or behind you. You see them from every angle and from every point of the compass. All that day we had them with us, and it seemed as if we should never get away from them."

William Bliss,
The Heart of England by Waterway, 1933

Rodney's Pillar

Rodney's Pillar was erected in 1782, the year when Admiral Sir George Brydges Rodney (1719–92) defeated the French off the island of Dominica in the Caribbean. The battle was a rare British victory in the American War of Independence. The monument was also a tribute to Montgomeryshire's contribution in supplying timber for naval ships. The sixteen-metre column was originally crowned by a gilded ball, destroyed by lightning. It is currently fenced off, in need of major repair to preserve it.

Trekking up to Rodney's Pillar from the river is recommended as an excellent morning or afternoon's diversion. Various footpaths lead from the river upstream of Llandrinio Bridge, to ascend Breidden Hill through forests on its east side. The view from the summit, also the site of an Iron Age hillfort, is stupendous; the river and plain stretch out 300m below you. Incidentally, Rodney's Pillar is nothing to do with Lord Hereford's Knob which overlooks the River Wye, so I am not sure why I even mentioned this.

Offa's Dyke Path National Trail has followed the river left bank since the launch point at Pool Quay. Offa's Dyke was constructed c784 / 5 as a boundary between Powys and Offa's Mercian kingdom, however it was never a continuous barrier and no earthwork traces have been found alongside the Severn. Four kilometres before Llandrinio Bridge, the National Trail departs the river to head north; this point is fifteen kilometres, although it feels much further, from the Pool Quay launch spot. Llandrinio Bridge has spanned the river in three, graceful arches since 1775. The bridge notably peaks in height at the central arch – lovely! Traces of a Roman crossing have been discovered at this out-of-the-way spot. Llandrinio is barely a village, a few houses around the twelfth century St Trinio's Church with

Llandrinio Bridge.

its odd, part-timber bell tower. The campsite here is a great spot at which to break up a trip and perhaps explore Breidden Hill.

A (relatively) steep rapid is funnelled beneath Llandrinio Bridge. The last five kilometres of the Welsh river wind tightly, a hangover from the 'squirrelly' stretch upstream of Llandrinio. Flood defence earthworks hem in the views

Weir Head.

but as Arthur Granville Bradley noted, the impossible-to-escape Breidden Hills still loom, *"like a pair of huge sentinels ... guarding the gateway from the plains of north Shropshire into the hills of Wales."* (The Rivers and Streams of England, 1909).

"The river here is beautiful, in a much more open valley of meadows hung with woods and copses ... It runs now and again between high banks with hills on either hand, but always with a view, and is extraordinarily picturesque."

William Bliss, *The Heart of England by Waterway*, 1933

Crewgreen.

You won't miss the Wales / England border; it is marked by the confluence on river left of a major tributary, the River Vyrnwy / Afon Efyrnwy. The two rivers are hard to distinguish in size (*Vyrnwy* actually derives from 'Severn') and this marks an immediate change in the Severn's character; *"now a 'goodly river', both as regards the volume of its waters and the beauty of the scenery on either bank"* (Great Western Railway, *The Severn Valley* 1923).

For two kilometres, the river left bank is England and river right is Wales. The border is straddled by the dilapidated and overgrown girders of Crewgreen Bridge. This has been a road bridge since 1962, but was built in 1942 as a rail bridge to carry war materials to the Shropshore and Montgomeryshire Line.

The Severn now enters England proper ... and there is absolutely nothing to see for the following fifteen kilometres! This isn't quite true, of course; nature supplies plenty of sights to enjoy (especially if you like willow trees) but the river winds, free of outside intrusion, with roads and villages distant or hidden from sight. A brief interlude of urban madness is supplied when you pass the tiny villages of Little Shrawardine on river right and Shrawardine on river left. You probably won't even spot Little Shrawardine and its motte-and-bailey castle overlooking the river, but Shrawardine is marked by a single cottage down at river level. Shrawardine also hosted a castle, 400m from the river; only the mound, ditch and traces of stonework survive as it was dismantled in 1645 by Cromwell's troops following a five-day siege.

"After Shrawardine the river itself becomes much more interesting ... glimpses of the lovely country on either hand become more frequent, with here and there the square red tower of the church to show the existence of a village that otherwise would hardly be seen."

Geoffrey Boumphrey, *Down River*, 1936

Boumphrey also noticed a change in the geology; *"on the south bank a quite new type of country appears – a high bank of trees, so steep in places as to show a vertical face of red sandstone."*

Shrawardine.

This Triassic sandstone, often forming cliffs along the outside of bends, is a recurrent feature of the river all the way down to the tidal reaches.

You might possibly glimpse the square tower of St Chad's on river left, marking the village of Montford. Charles Darwin's parents Robert Darwin and Susannah Wedgwood (daughter of the potter Josiah) are buried here, along with his sister. Montford's proximity is also marked by a small rapid passing a large island at The Weir. The island was artificially created to bypass the fish weir that existed here from the eleventh century until removal in the nineteenth.

Extended, left bends below wooded slopes indicate that you're passing Preston Montford, where a seventeenth century country house is now a field studies centre. You'll first hear the A5 and then spot the concrete Montford Bypass Bridge. Until this was built in 1992, all traffic for North Wales squeezed through the village of Montford Bridge, 350m downstream. Montford Bridge's bridge(!) was designed by Thomas Telford and built by John Carline and John Tilley in 1792, using red sandstone quarried at Nesscliffe. A white, octagonal, toll house guards the river left end. There has been a bridge here since at least 1283, when Dafydd ap Gruffudd, the last true Prince of Wales, was handed over to the English at the crossing. He was brutally hung, drawn and quartered at Shrewsbury, on the orders of Edward I.

Take out just above the bridge on river right.

The Isle

Montford Bridge.

Section 7

Montford Bridge to Shrewsbury

Distance 22.2km
Start △ Montford Bridge SJ 432 152 / SY4 1EB
Finish ◯ Shrewsbury Weir SJ 500 130 / SY1 2JW

Introduction

*"High the vanes of Shrewsbury gleam
Islanded in Severn stream."*

A. E. Housman, *A Shropshire Lad*, 1896

The Severn, now a sizeable river, swoops from one wooded scarp to another, apparently having decided to up its game and put on some pace to reach Shrewsbury. The glorious solitude of the first part is followed by an interesting float through the historic town.

Launch points

Montford Bridge (Wingfield Caravan Park) SJ 432 152 / SY4 1EB – river right, above Montford Bridge's bridge. Parking area behind the Wingfield Arms. Only with prior arrangement and payment of a launching fee.

Shrewsbury (Frankwell Footbridge) SJ 490 128 / SY3 8HQ – river right. Various places to land up- and downstream of the bridge, alongside Frankwell car park.

Shrewsbury (Shrewsbury Weir) SJ 500 130 / SY1 2JW – river left. Free riverside parking at the end of Burton Street, beside Shrewsbury Weir toilets and along Sydney Avenue. Go through a gate to launch below the weir.

Description

What a magnificent stretch of river this is! Leaving Montford Bridge, you immediately enter the Shropshire wilds; the Severn flows for seventeen kilometres to Shrewsbury with – like Section 6 – few signs of outside life. The flow is often swift and regular, riffly rapids maintain interest.

After two kilometres the River Perry joins from river left, just past an island. This tiny tributary is barely noticeable or worthy of mention ... except that it has been used, amazingly, by open canoe supremos Rob Egelstaff and Ray Goodwin to reach the Severn from the Shropshire Union Canal and complete a 'circumnavigation' of Wales.

The remarkable feature of this whole section is The Isle, where the Severn describes an enormous, eight-kilometre loop, doubling back on itself to pass just 300m from its start point. The land enclosed is the Isle Estate, 350

The Isle.

hectares of farmland. The 'neck' of The Isle, occupied by Isle Grange (hidden from view), was once crossed by a sluice tunnel which powered a flannel mill at the downhill end.

Around The Isle and beyond, broad sweeping bends are backed by wooded scarps, overlooking farmland on the opposite bank. There are no notable landmarks and without careful map perusal, you will struggle to keep track of your location. The first signs that you are approaching Shrewsbury are occasional glimpses of buildings high on the river right bank, above the slopes known as Shelton Rough. Following this, a sharp left and then a long right bend (Laundry Terrace) are worth looking out for, as just downstream, the banks lower in height and the river right bank becomes Doctor's Field Countryside Heritage Site. This is Charles Darwin's birthplace! He was born in 1809 at The Mount, 120m from the river. To encourage young Darwin to engage with nature, his father created a 'thinking path' which wound around Doctor's Field and along the riverbank.

The Severn follows a tight right bend around a recreation ground at Mountfields, entering the

Laundry Terrace, approaching Shrewsbury.

Entering Shrewsbury.

The Quantum Leap, Shrewsbury.

town proper. Frankwell Footbridge, a cable-stay suspension bridge, is an ideal place to finish if you don't want to continue through the town. There are various options to land on river right, the last being a public slipway on Frankland Quay near the Theatre Severn.

Shrewsbury originated on the promontory which the Severn tightly encircles with a three-kilometre loop. There are eight bridges in this distance, the main crossings being the Welsh and English Bridges which formerly carried the London-Holyhead Road through town, making Shrewsbury the literal gateway into Wales. The Welsh Bridge is directly downstream of Frankwell Footbridge; five arches span 81 metres in total, the work of John Carline and John Tilley in 1795. Mardol Quay, on river left above the Welsh Bridge, is home to The Quantum Leap, an abstract sculpture unveiled in 2009 to commemorate the bicentenary of Darwin's birth. It resembles a twisting backbone, or perhaps a segment of DNA; but it has been nicknamed 'The Slinky' by detractors and eyebrows were raised by the million-pound price tag.

Medieval Shrewsbury

"Shrewsbury is a most interesting town and, as the gateway to Wales, it has a long and stormy history, which is portrayed to a certain extent in its buildings and ruins ... the canoeist will find that a halt here for sightseeing will be well repaid"

Alec R. Ellis, *The Book of Canoeing*, 1935

Shrewsbury emerged as a stronghold on the loop in the Severn after the decline of Roman Virconium (page 107). Through the Early Medieval period, the town was called Pengwern (capital of a Saxon kingdom), Scrobbesbyrig, Amwythig (Welsh), Salopia and Schrosberie! The castle and abbey were built following the Norman Conquest, when Shrewsbury became a Marcher lordship: a buffer zone against the Welsh. The town's wealth grew from control of the Welsh wool trade.

Shrewsbury is possibly Britain's best-preserved Medieval town, with 660 listed buildings lining half-timbered streets like Wyle Cop, connected by narrow passages known as shuts and gulleys.

Below Welsh Bridge, the Sabrina tour boat is moored on river left at Victoria Quay. It's only 450m to Porthill Suspension Bridge, an ornate 1922 footbridge which is one of several suspension bridges built on the Severn by David Rowell & Co. The half-timbered Boathouse Inn guards this former ferry crossing on river right; it housed plague victims in the seventeenth century. National Cycle Route 81 crosses the bridge and follows the river left bank through town and past Shrewsbury Weir. The Severn bends left around The Quarry, a public park which contains The Dingle ornamental gardens and is used for events such as the Shrewsbury Flower Show (a rock concert was underway when we last paddled past). The Quarry is backed by Saint Chad's, a highly distinctive and unusual church. George Steuart combined Doric and Corinthian influences to design the 46m-high, cupola tower and 30m diameter circular nave, opened in 1792. The hillside overlooking Quarry Park on river right is topped by imposing Shrewsbury School (2020 Independent School of the Year, apparently). On the river front are two historic boathouses; Pengwern Boathouse (distinguished by its half-timbered gable) was built in 1881, housing Pengwern Boat Club who were established in the year that Shrewsbury Regatta first took place, 1871. Shrewsbury School's rowing club is older (established 1866) but their boathouse was built in 1921 as a memorial to the school's First World War losses.

More bridges! John William Glover's Kingsland Bridge dates from 1883, a toll bridge

Pengwern Boathouse and Shrewsbury School.

Upstream of Shrewsbury Weir.

supported by a lone 65m steel arch. Greyfriars Footbridge (opened 1879) is a lattice of girders, and then a sharp left bend (where Rea Brook joins on river right) leads to English Bridge. John Gwynne's seven arches span 120m, completed in 1774 at a cost of £15,710. Gywnne's tall design was lowered and doubled in width in a 1920s rebuild, so pontists will have to visit his Atcham Bridge (Section 8) to glory in his unadulterated vision.

English Bridge was constructed across an island, and several sandy islets survive downstream, occupied by nesting swans. The river right bank is the Abbey Gardens; site of Shrewsbury Abbey and location of Ellis Peters' Brother Cadfael 'whodunnit' novels. Only the church survives now, some way back from the river. The river left bank is overshadowed by rather grim apartment blocks, backed by the spire of St Mary's Church.

Shrewsbury Castle looms on river left, upstream of Shrewsbury Railway Station Bridge. The red sandstone castle you see today was rebuilt in

Robert Cadman, aviator

A plaque on the tower of St Mary's Church tells the story of early aviator Robert Cadman. In 1739 he rigged some form of zipwire from the 68-metre spire, in order to 'fly' across the Severn ...

'From a bold attempt to fly from this high spire,
Across the Sabrine stream, he did acquire
His fatal end; 'twas not for want of skill,
Or courage to perform the task, he fell;
No, no, a faulty cord, being drawn too tight ...'
He is buried in the churchyard.

Wilfred Owen and Shrewsbury

War poet Wilfred Owen (*'Dulce et Decorum Est'*) grew up 200m from Shrewsbury Weir; his blue-plaqued home at 69 Monkmoor Road is a five-minute walk from the park on river right. His family would walk to Uffington Church via the Uffington ferry crossing; the memory of yellow pollen clinging to his shoes is referenced in the poem *'Spring Offensive'*. Owen is commemorated by an abstract sculpture 'Symmetry' in the grounds of Shrewsbury Abbey. It was inaugurated in 1993, the centenary of his birthday, with the inscription 'I AM THE ENEMY YOU KILLED MY FRIEND' from his poem *'Strange Meeting'*.

Owen is buried at Ors in France; he was killed a week before the end of the First World War.

---

the 1780s by Thomas Telford, for Sir William Pulteney MP. It originated in 1070 as a motte-and-bailey, the base of Roger de Montgomery, first Earl of Shrewsbury. It expanded in the twelfth and thirteenth centuries to become a Royal fortress under Henry II. It held for the king during the English Civil War and subsequently fell into ruin, until Telford got to work; his notable addition was Laura's Tower, the prominent viewpoint overlooking the river.

Shrewsbury Railway Station Bridge is a grimy monster, its gloomy expanse explained by the fact that it literally supports the railway station above. Shortly after emerging from the dark tunnels beneath, you reach Castle Walk Footbridge; built in 1951, this was Britain's first pre-stressed concrete, balanced cantilever bridge … although I honestly have no clue what that means. Anyway, Shrewsbury Weir looms a short distance downstream, so it is time to select a spot to climb out on river left.

Variations

It's possible to explore upstream on the River Vyrnwy. 1.5 kilometres from the confluence with the Severn is the village of Melverley, where the remarkable St Peter's Church overlooks the river. The church dates from pre-1406 and is of timber-framed wattle and daub construction, painted black-and-white.

Near Wroxeter.

St Eata's Church, Atcham.

© Ismore Coppice.

Section 8

Shrewsbury to Ironbridge

Distance 34.1km
Start △ Shrewsbury Weir, Shrewsbury SJ 500 130 / SY1 2JW
Finish ◯ Dale End Park, Ironbridge SJ 665 036 / TF8 7DG

Introduction

"The Severn writhes like an eel where the Wrekin casts its shadow over the green fields, as the monumental hill forces the river through the Wenlock Edge into the half industrial, half romantic gorge of Ironbridge."

Brian Waters in *Portraits of Rivers*, 1953
Downstream of Shrewsbury, the Severn is in no particular hurry as it snakes across the plain, approaching Wenlock Edge and Ironbridge Gorge. The scenery is always attractive and there are lots of interesting things to see along the route.

Launch points

Shrewsbury (Shrewsbury Weir) SJ 500 130 / SY1 2JW – river left. Free riverside parking at the end of Burton Street beside Shrewsbury Weir toilets and along Sydney Avenue. Go through a gate to launch below the weir.

Atcham Bridges SJ 540 093 / SY5 6QH – park in the layby beside the B4380 on the river right side of the bridges. Cross the lane to the path leading to Old Atcham Bridge (the pedestrian bridge). Just before the bridge, a rough path leads down to the river on the left, between the bridges. The easiest launch spot

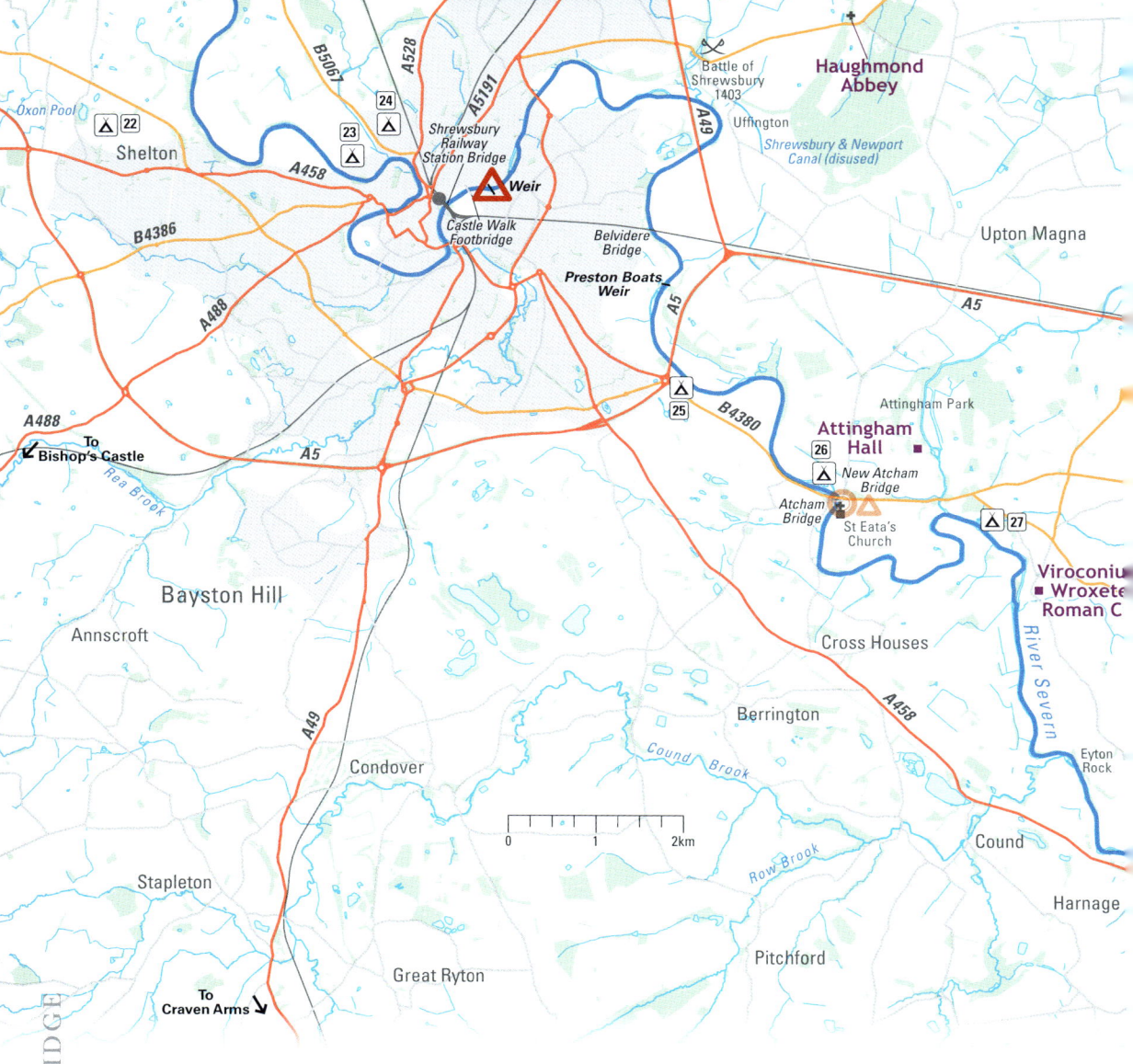

is reached through a tunnel in the old bridge! There is alternatively, a path leading down from the bridge on the right to a beach; this is a popular spot but skirts private land.

Cressage Bridge SJ 594 045 / SY5 6BZ – river left, launch upstream of bridge from public footpath. Very limited parking, room for one car at best.

Buildwas SJ 648 044 / TF8 7BN – river left. Very limited parking in small layby on Buildwas Road. Follow the public footpath 150m down to a beach.

Ironbridge (Dale End Park) SJ 665 036 / TF8 7DG – river left. Dale End car park in Dale End Park. Riverside car park and slipways, off The Wharfage. There is also Wharfage car park 100m further downstream, but at time of writing paddlers here are being challenged by

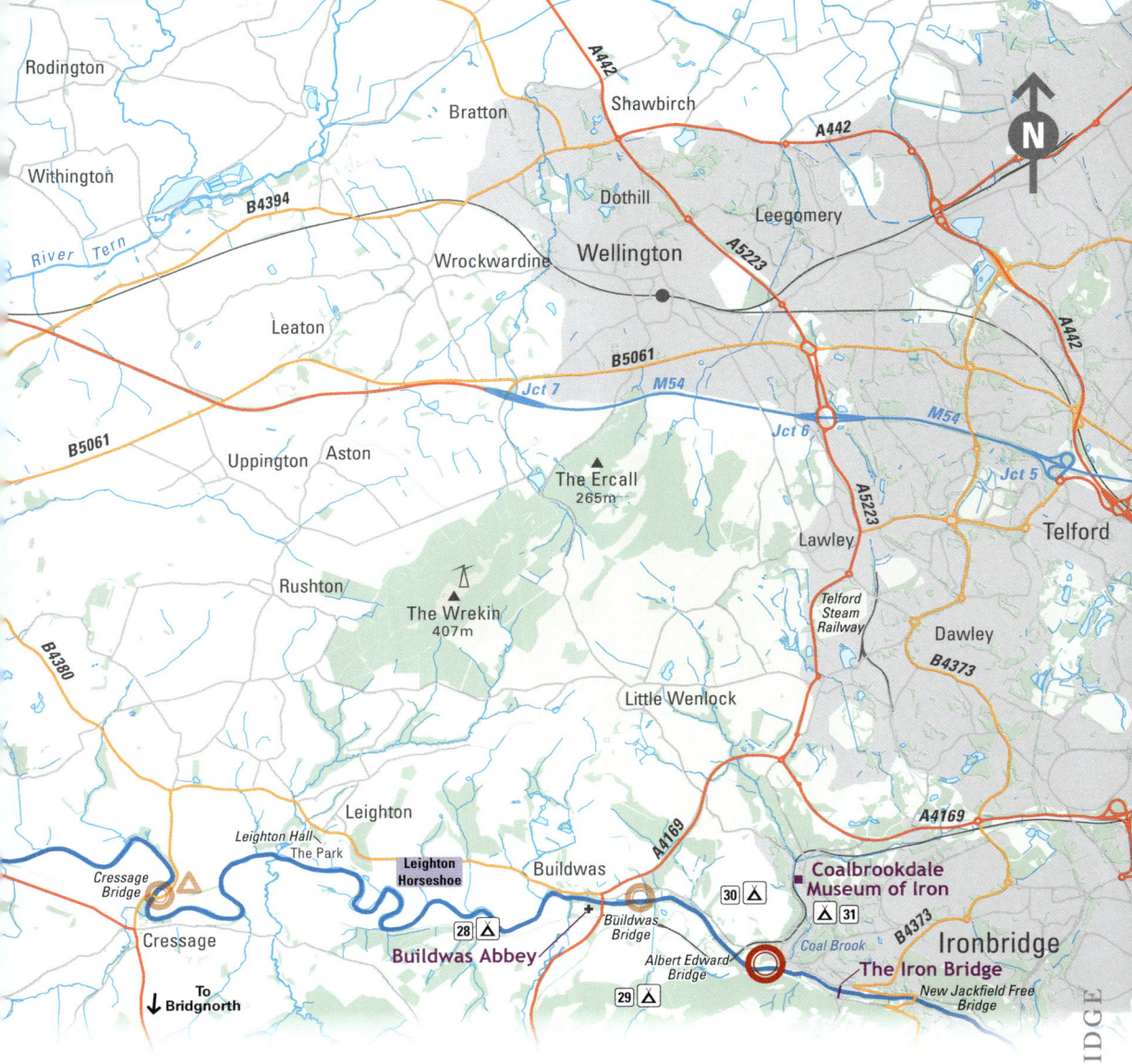

a canoe / raft hire company, who claim to control access to the river; ludicrous, obviously.

Description

This long day out could be divided into two at Atcham, although landing and launching there is awkward. Another possible approach is a camp at idyllic Ismore Coppice Wild Campground.

Shrewsbury Weir is paddleable by those with white water know-how, in low flows; otherwise, launch below. The remainder of Shrewsbury is largely hidden from view as you depart the town through parkland and past a long island, site of a former fish weir. However, over the next eight kilometres four successive high and hefty concrete road bridges serving the town intrude, cropping up

Belvidere Bridge.

at intervals whenever you think that you've finally escaped Shrewsbury. The first carries the A5112 at Ditherington. 2.5km downstream, just after the first of many small rapids alongside islands, the A49 rudely intrudes overhead, and then crosses again shortly after. Between these A49 bridges, the Severn bends right passing the village of Uffington on river left. It's worth landing for lunch at The Corbet Arms, and walking 1.5km following the Shropshire Way across the Shrewsbury and Newport Canal (disused, undergoing restoration) and along Haughmond Hill to explore Haughmond Abbey. This impressive, twelfth-century ruin is managed by English Heritage. Uffington is the spot where in 1403, King Henry IV forded the river to defeat the army of Harry Hotspur (Henry Percy) near Haughmond Abbey.

Centuries after the Battle of Shrewsbury, a young Charles Darwin recorded finding, *"a surprising number of iron arrowheads ... on the northern side of the Severn."*

Belvidere Bridge consists of two cast iron arches carrying Shrewsbury's main rail link, overlooking a small rapid. Shortly below around a right bend, a former ferry house on river left is followed by Preston Boats Weir. This former fish weir drops a miniscule height but is ancient enough to be mentioned in the *Domesday Book* and belonged to Haughmond Abbey. It was the last in use on the river, with a complex structure of oak piles and wattle panels. Alec R. Ellis described, *"stakes and wires across the river"* in his 1935 *The Book of Canoeing*. Amazingly, the weir's zig-zag design (to funnel eels into nets) is still clearly marked out by the shallow bank of stones. The long island stretching below is a remnant of the osier (willow) islands which were harvested around weirs.

The roaring A5 bridge is the last of Shrewsbury's intrusions. The river continues to be characterised by deep, winding reaches, interspersed by shallow, riffly rapids, often alongside islands and the sites of former fish weirs. Having just escaped Shrewsbury's irritating, concrete bridges, it's ironic that the most attractive landmark now is … another bridge. New Atcham Bridge is inoffensive enough, opened in 1929 with a design by L. G. Mouchel. However, directly adjacent is John Gwynne's 1776 Atcham Bridge, seven arches (home to house martins) and a 124m span, built in a neo-classical style to complement nearby Attingham Hall. The bridge has been preserved in its original narrow form (now a footbridge), unlike Gwynne's English Bridge (Shrewsbury) and Worcester Bridge. It's a contender for the most attractive bridge on the entire river, backdropped by the Mytton and Mermaid Hotel (an eighteenth-century coaching inn) and the tower of St Eata's Church, both on river left.

St Eata was a seventh-century, Celtic saint. The only church dedicated to him looms over the rapid below the bridges, constructed from dark red sandstone (pilfered from Viroconium, see below). There has been a church on the site since the eighth century, but the present structure originates from the eleventh century, with the inevitable nineteenth century restorations. The chronicler Orderic Vitalis

 *Atcham Bridges.*

Approaching Ismore Coppice.

(1075–1142) was baptised here. The tower's spire was destroyed by lightning in 1879; Shrewsbury Museum possesses several of the choirboy's boots, fused by the bolt!

"It would be hard to find a better bit of England than the stretch from Atcham to Buildwas. The Wrekin, with its wooded flanks, to the north, standing upon the farther slopes that sweep down with sturdy wood and quiet green fields to the river. On the right the land climbs up to where Wenlock Edge starts."

Geoffrey Boumphrey, *Down River*, 1936

Five winding kilometres with regular riffles and rapids lead towards (and sometimes away from) the village of Wroxeter. The confluence of the River Tern on river left (note the remains of a former lock) indicates that you are passing Attingham Park, a hundred-hectare deer park landscaped by Humphrey Repton. The National Trust now own the park and neo-classical Attingham Hall, designed by George Steuart and completed in 1785. A stay at the NT's splendidly low-key Ismore Coppice Wild Campground (signposted on river left) is recommended to fully explore Attingham Park and also the Roman city of Viroconium, which

Ismore Coppice campsite.

Viroconium

Viroconium, 'Wroxeter Roman City', covered 80 hectares and was the fourth largest Roman city in Britain. It originated in the late 50s AD as a garrison town to control the Cornovii tribe (based at the Wrekin) and the river crossing at the terminus of Watling Street. After the legions relocated to Chester in 90 AD, it developed into a city. This thrived well enough to remain in use following the Roman withdrawal (c410AD), but was abandoned by the seventh century AD. Only a fraction of this vast site has been excavated; in the 1920s archaeologists uncovered the central forum, market hall and baths. 'The Old Work' still stands at the heart of this, a seven-metre basilica wall which is the highest surviving civilian building in Britain. These ruins can be explored via an English Heritage museum and recreated town house.

occupied the river left bank for 1.5km past the campsite. Traces of a wooden Roman bridge have been uncovered at the island which follows the campground. Passing the island, you might spy St Andrew's Church at Wroxeter (a tiny village on river left), whose nave, gate posts and font clearly originate from the Roman ruins.

The seven kilometres from Wroxeter to Cressage Bridge flow straighter. The confluence of Cound Brook on river right is followed by islands and a rapid, and then Eytonrock on river left, a small sandstone cliff. The Severn bends sharp left at Cound, leading into yet another island riffle and overlooked by the Riverside Inn.

Cressage Bridge crosses via three concrete spans designed by L.G Mouchel; built in 1913, it replaced Telford's eighteenth-century, timber, trestle bridge. Incidentally, 'Cressage' derives from *Christ's oak*; this is reputedly where St Augustine preached to Welsh priests in 584, under an oak tree. The bridge marks a noticeable change in the landscape, with the sides of valley drawing closer. The wooded ridge of Wenlock Edge is on river right and Thomas Harral noted, *"at Cressage Bridge ... the Wrekin forms a fine and conspicuous object in the view"* (*Picturesque Views of the Severn*, 1824). If you look back upstream, you enjoy your first view of the Wrekin which henceforth looms on river left. This Shropshire landmark is unmistakeable; a steep-sided and tree-covered, 407m-high, volcanic plug rears from the plain, topped by an Iron Age hillfort and, latterly, a communications mast.

Eytonrock.

📷 *The Wrekin.*

"We were hardly ever out of sight of the Wrekin, to left, right, ahead or behind us, as the river twisted and turned before entering the Ironbridge Gorge which it cut for itself at the end of the Great Ice Age."

Geoffrey Boumphrey, *Down River*, 1936

As the Severn draws closer to squeezing through Wenlock Edge via Ironbridge Gorge, it counterintuitively slows down! There are numerous meanders and the river widens approaching the gorge (5km away, but an 8km paddle). The vista ahead was long dominated by the four cooling towers and 204m chimney of Ironbridge Power Station. The towers were demolished in 2019 and the chimney in 2021, transforming and restoring the landscape.

Sheinton Brook enters on river right and the river left bank is open fields ('The Park') fronting Leighton Hall, birthplace of Shropshire novelist Mary Webb. The hillside upon which it sits is Leighton Bank, with the Wrekin peeking over from behind. The following meanders (known as Leighton Horseshoe) are a chance to enjoy these vistas, framed behind high earth banks colonised by sand martins.

A few houses perched on river left indicate that you are passing Buildwas, and shortly beyond is Buildwas Bridge. This unprepossessing 1992 road bridge is the third on the site, the previous two having been damaged by earth movements. Buildwas Abbey is directly alongside the river right shore, but this attractive ruin is not visible or easily accessible from the water and is probably best saved for a land-based visit.

The steep hillsides rising behind both banks

The ruins of Buildwas

Buildwas Abbey was founded in 1135 as part of the Savignac Order, which merged with the Cistercians in 1147. Buildwas was a 'daughter house' of Furness Abbey in Cumbria but visiting the towering remains, including an imposing Romanesque columned nave, you'll see that it was anything but second-rate. The monks' wealth was accrued by charging bridge tolls, trading wool downriver river to Bristol and then France, and even running their own ironworks. Their affluence did not go unnoticed, and the abbey was dissolved in 1536; folk visiting picturesque, ruined monasteries often don't realise that they are in ruins not because of the ravages of time but because Henry VIII's greedy commissioners stripped them of *everything*, including the roof lead and window glass. Although it is directly alongside the Severn, the Abbey can only be accessed via the English Heritage entrance, 100m south of Buildwas Bridge.

make it obvious that you've finally entered Ironbridge Gorge. The river narrows and flows more determinedly, passing beneath three successive bridges which served the Ironbridge Power Stations. These closed in 2015 and the site is being redeveloped with a school and housing. Opposite the power stations is the site of a major landslide! In 1773, an earthquake caused ten hectares of green fields to divert the river's course. The Vicar of Madeley preached on the brink of the ten-metre chasm through which the Severn now surged, *"You walk today on solid ground where fishes yesterday swam in twenty feet of water ... Ye profane watermen, whose daring wickedness overflows all the dikes of human and profane laws, oftener than the Severn does its banks; see what a curse has overtaken the river on which you earn your bread."*
Ironbridge Gorge has no sheer sides today (despite the name), but the landslip is an indication of how this relatively young landscape is far from stable.

The third bridge passing the power station site is the attractive 61m span of Albert Edward Bridge, opened in 1864 in honour of Queen Victoria's son. A twin of Victoria Bridge near Arley (Section 10), it was designed by Sir John Fowler and constructed using cast iron from the Coalbrookdale Iron Company's foundries, just a kilometre away. Ironbridge Rowing Club is just past the bridge, on river left.

"At the foot of Benthall Edge, the railway crosses the river by a bridge 200-foot in span, and brings before us, at a glance, this interesting little valley ... The name has long been famous, as well for its romantic scenery as for its ironworks."

John Randall,
Handbook of the Severn Valley Railway, 1863
Albert Edward Bridge marks the point at which the River Severn enters the Ironbridge Gorge World Heritage Site ... a far more famous iron bridge awaits just a short distance downstream! However, before this is seen you reach the ramp on river left which leads up to Dale End car park.

High Rock, Bridgnorth.

Ironbridge. Photo | James Appleton.

Section 9

Ironbridge to Bridgnorth

Distance 14.3km
Start △ Dale End Park, Ironbridge SJ 665 036 / TF8 7DG
Finish ○ Severn Park, Bridgnorth SO 719 933 / WV15 5AF

Introduction

"A winding glen ... hemmed in by lofty hills and hanging woods"

Samuel Bagshaw, *History, Gazetteer, and Directory of Shropshire*, 1851

A stunning paddle through (rewilded) industrial heritage followed by a surprisingly remote deep valley, with the notable challenge of Jackfield Rapids to paddle or portage.

Launch points

Ironbridge (Dale End Park) SJ 665 036 / TF8 7DG – river left. Dale End car park in Dale End Park. Riverside car park and slipways, off The Wharfage. There is also Wharfage car park 100m further downstream, but at time of writing paddlers here are being challenged by a canoe / raft hire company, who claim to control access to the river; ludicrous, obviously.

Jackfield (Half Moon Inn) SJ 690 028 / TF8 7LP – river right, slipway and pub car park. 'Patrons Only', seek permission from Half Moon Inn.

Coalport (Jackfield & Coalport Memorial Bridge) SJ 693 026 / TF8 7HR – river left, just upstream of bridge. Parking area accessed by small side road leading uphill from Coalport High Street. Steep / awkward access to the river.

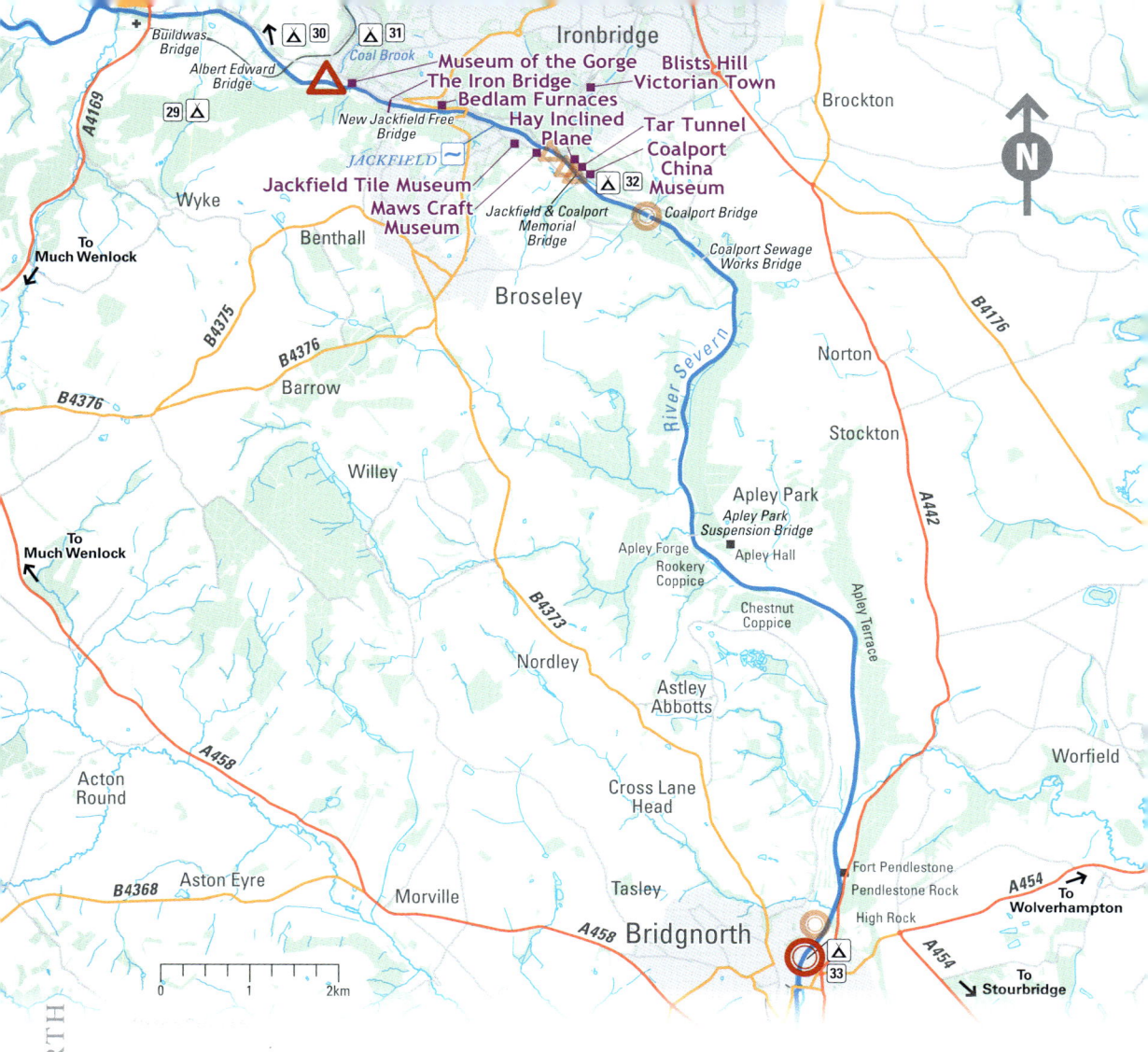

Jackfield (Boat Inn) SJ 693 025 / TF8 7HS – river right, just downstream of Jackfield & Coalport Memorial Bridge. Parking beside Memorial Tree. Launch spot is accessed through the pub's beer garden, seek permission.

Coalport (Coalport Bridge) SJ 701 021 / TF8 7JA – river left, just upstream of bridge. Parking is very limited, either beside bridge itself or near private road on right just past The Brewery Inn.

Bridgnorth (Southwell Riverside) SO 720 935 / WV16 4JZ – riverside parking on Southwell Riverside, river right and upstream of Bridgnorth Bridge. Free parking for two hours only, unload and leave car in a side street.

Bridgnorth (Severn Park) SO 719 933 / WV15 5AF – large public park with riverside parking, on river left upstream of Bridgnorth Bridge. Large slipway and other points at which the water can be accessed.

The Iron Bridge.

Description

The stream trickling into the Severn at the put-in is Coal Brook, which gives its name to Coalbrookdale. Coalbrookdale is where the industrial breakthroughs which made the area world-famous commenced, however the district is now named and better known for the Iron Bridge, opened in 1779 to showcase these achievements; welcome to Ironbridge Gorge, a UNESCO World Heritage Site! The extraordinary thing is just how much the area has recovered from the (comparatively recent) ravages of industry and regreened with limestone woodlands.

The first landmark, reached immediately on river left, is the Museum of the Gorge. This peculiar, neo-Gothic, redbrick building was formerly the Coalbrookdale Company Warehouse. A horse-drawn plateway linked the furnaces in Coalbrookdale to the wharf here, where 60-ton trows (barges) were loaded. The road above the river left bank is still called The Wharfage and the opposite bank is Bower Yard, where shipbuilding took place; in 1756, 139 boats were owned in the gorge!

The Iron Bridge is just 450m downstream. The world's first single-span, iron bridge was lauded as *"One of the wonders of the world"* by Viscount Torrington shortly after its opening, and this icon of the Industrial Revolution still has the power to awe. Take time whilst drifting beneath the high rust-red arches to marvel at the construction methods; the bridge was slotted together in kit form from nearly 1700 individual parts, using what were essentially woodworking techniques.

In the 1850s Matthew Webb, son of a Coalbrookdale doctor, learned to swim here and even saved his brother from drowning beneath the Iron Bridge. In 1875 he achieved world fame as the first to swim the English Channel. High on the river left end of the bridge, the tourist shops and cafes of Ironbridge are overlooked by St Luke's; this 1837 church unusually has its tower at the east end, due to the unstable ground. Although you are not far into your trip, it is possible to land at steps just upstream of the bridge and climb up to explore the town.

The Severn remains narrow and hemmed in by steep wooded banks, as the Gorge continues.

The stretch immediately below Ironbridge is delightful, fast-flowing over rocky reefs with kingfishers commonly spotted. Well into the twentieth century, this was the domain of oval-shaped coracles which ferried people cross-river to avoid the bridge toll and were also notoriously used for poaching game by night, all the way down to Bridgnorth.

A long rapid leads towards New Jackfield Free Bridge, a striking 'asymmetric cable stay' design supported by an impressive slanting 30m steel tower. It was built in 1994 after L. G. Mouchel's 'Old' Free Bridge of 1909 became unsafe; a section of this is preserved, alongside a plaque.

The Iron Bridge

"The bridge itself makes a light & elegant appearance tho' apparently no ways deficient in strength. In viewing it either up or down water it resembles an elegant Arch in some ancient Cathedral."

Samuel Butler, *Diary*, 1782

Abraham Darby III cast the Iron Bridge 1777-1779, from a design by Thomas Farnolls Pritchard (d1777), at a cost of £5,000. The core of the bridge is five 21m ribs, each weighing over five tonnes, supporting a carriageway of cast iron plates above a single 60m span, 15m clear of the water to allow sailing boats through. The whole structure weighs in at about 350 tonnes, and the unstable, local geology has struggled to support it. The bridge was closed to traffic from the 1930s due to buckling stresses from the shifting banks and underwent major restoration and renovation in 2000.

What was it for? It obviously connected the districts of Coalbrookdale and Broseley (albeit charging a toll) but the real reason for Darby III's extravagant creation was to show off the Darby dynasty's achievements in iron-making and the potential of their product. The Iron Bridge was a large, brash, unmissable advert, *"a stupendous specimen of the powers of mechanism"* (John Pinkerton, *A General Collection of Best and Most Interesting Voyages and Travels in All Parts of the World*, 1808). It was a success in this sense, drawing visitors (and customers) from around the globe and transforming Coalbrookdale into 'Ironbridge', promoted in 1876 as, *"the Brighton of the Midland counties"* by a local hotelier.

Careful now, as things happen fast; Jackfield Rapids are a short distance downstream of the bridge. By the time you spot the garden of the Black Swan pub on river right, you're almost committed to running them! If you are unfamiliar with the rapids you need to quickly land on the rocky river left bank and use the paths along the shore to inspect.

"These are the most serious, the only serious, falls on the Severn, and in low water can be very awkward."

William Bliss, Canoeing, 1934

Jackfield is indeed a 'proper' white water rapid, unlike anything else along the English Severn's course (except, possibly, Folly Point Rapids in Section 10). Large boulders channel jets of water, forming waves and small stoppers, with a noticeable drop in height: grade 3. The rapids were formed by landslips and waste dumped down the banks, and have changed many times over the years; for example, a 1952 landslip devastated part of Jackfield village and narrowed the river by fifteen metres. The banks were stabilised in 2014 and rocks have been shifted to engineer a decent white water training and slalom site, lined by eddies. In very low flows, a central rock diverts the flow, in high flows all is submerged and you just encounter bouncy waves.

"If you lack confidence in your ability to manage the rapids you can always carry around."

W.G. Luscombe and L.J. Bird, Canoeing, 1948

Portaging is simple enough following the river left paths down to the beach at the rapids' end, however there is no simple exit point

Jackfield Rapids.

upstream of the rapids and a rope may prove helpful to lift your paddlecraft up the large boulders stabilising the bank. Incidentally, the rapids have existed for centuries; they were known as 'The Coals' by bargemen.

Jackfield itself, lining the river right bank, was formerly a riverport, exporting coal, earthenware pottery and tiles. This was the site of the largest encaustic tile works in the world, today recalled by Jackfield Tile Museum and Maws Craft Centre. Paddlers scanning the beaches downstream to Bridgnorth will find that they are largely comprised of tile remnants ('wasters'), often decorated!

The Jackfield and Coalport Memorial Footbridge was built in 1922, funded by public subscription to commemorate the fallen of the First World War. It connects the Boat Inn in Jackfield to the Shakespeare Inn in Coalport (river left), on the site of the Coalport ferry. In 1799, this capsized and 28 people drowned: *"It was a dark night, the boat was crowded ... with a strong tide running, it was drawn under."* (John Randall, *The Clay Industries*, 1877).

Coalport was a key component of the Ironbridge Gorge industries, being *"... very advantageously situated, having the river, the canal, and two railways adjoining"* (John Randall, *Handbook of the Severn Valley Railway*, 1863). The remarkable Hay Inclined Plane lifted floating tubs (filled with coal or iron) out of the lower canal alongside the Memorial Bridge, up a 1 in 3 gradient and into the Shropshire Canal (built 1788–92), 63m above. This and the Tar Tunnel, a 910m tunnel bored into the hillside to extract bitumen and now part

Coalport Bridge.

of the Coalport China Museum, can be visited by landing upstream of the Memorial Bridge. Coalport Bridge is an attractive cast iron span between supporting pillars, built in 1818 to replace a wooden bridge destroyed by ice floes in the epic flood of 1795. The bridge marks the end of Ironbridge Gorge, and the Severn leaves the World Heritage Site just downstream of the Woodbridge Inn which sits on river right.

The valley remains steep-sided and heavily wooded, with the Severn bubbling over frequent small rapids. After the unprepossessing Coalport Sewage Works Bridge is passed, the only outside intrusion comes from the river right shores; anglers, and the occasional walker or cyclist following the Severn Way / National Cycle Route 45 along the former course of the railway. The river left bank is frequently choked with fallen or trailing trees. Geoffrey Boumphrey appreciated this stretch: *"The six miles to Bridgnorth are through wonderful country; from the left banks woods rise without a break almost two hundred feet above the river; on the other side a quiet meadow or two throw open the view to even higher but more gently sloping hills to the west"* (*Down River*, 1936).

Apley Forge.

Apley Park Suspension Bridge (AKA Linley Bridge) is reached after four kilometres, a graceful, white-painted footbridge built in 1905 by David Rowell & Co. The Severn Valley Railway had to install the bridge as a condition of acquiring the land for Linley Station, uphill on river right; reputedly the owner of Apley Park wanted it to extend his fox hunts across the river. Apley Park sprawls along a hundred hectares of the river left valley side, around Apley Hall (not easily seen from the river, but dominating the view from the Severn Way footpath on the river right bank). Built in 1811 for Thomas Whitmore MP, this castellated, Gothic, stately pile was the largest and most expensive country house ever built in England. P.G. Wodehouse stayed here, and it was the inspiration for Blandings Castle, the location of his 'Jeeves and Wooster' stories.

"I do not think there can be a finer park in England, between an avenue of great horse-chestnut trees whose blossoms as we came down it that May noon were being blown upon the sunny water."

William Bliss,
The Heart of England by Waterway, 1933

Apley Park was open to the public in Victorian times, but is now private and Apley Hall has been converted into apartments (probably not in the 'affordable housing' category).

Directly below the bridge is Apley Forge, a few isolated cottages on river right which (as the name implies) was the site of two forges on Linley Brook, fuelled by wood coppiced from Rookery Coppice behind. Rookery Coppice leads into Chestnut Coppice, where the trees hide rock houses cut into sandstone cliffs, before the river flows beneath the soaring heights of Apley Terrace, 100m above the river left bank. The sandstone extends into the river as a series of shallow slabs forming mild rapids. This steep and densely wooded scarp follows the Severn into Bridgnorth, the trees occasionally parting to reveal the cliffs beneath.

"If there is a finer river view than this anywhere in England – or indeed in Europe – I do not know it."

William Bliss, *The Heart of England by Waterway*, 1933

Paddlers pass beneath two successive sandstone crags in the final kilometre to

The *Trial*

Apley Forge was the site where in 1787, to the accompaniment of cannon fire, John 'Iron-mad' Wilkinson launched the world's first iron boat *Trial*. In a letter he noted, *"Yesterday week my iron boat was launched; it answers all my expectations, and has convinced the unbelievers who were 999 in a 1,000."*

Arrival at Bridgnorth.

The Museum of the Gorge.

Bridgnorth, Pendlestone Rock and High Rock. The first looms above peculiar Fort Pendlestone, a forbidding, grey building which served as an ironworks for Abraham Darby III, was later a carpet factory and is now a private residence. High Rock (which is higher) rears right from the river and makes for a pretty grand entrance to the town.

The slipway at Severn Park is quickly reached on river left. Whatever else you do in Bridgnorth, take the funicular railway up the cliffs to High Town, for a tremendous view back along the stretch you just paddled.

Variations

If you just want to paddle and explore Ironbridge Gorge, it is probably easiest to launch at Dale End Park and simply paddle up- and downstream from this spot. If the river is flowing high however, it may be difficult to make progress back upstream. If you want to paddle Jackfield Rapids, there are a number of potential spots at which to egress below the rapids; these are outlined above, but check them out beforehand as none are straightforward.

Sights to see

Apart from the bridge itself, there are no end of industrial heritage sites to explore around Ironbridge. A simple and free start point is the Bedlam Furnaces (SJ 678 033 / TF8 7AA), the remains of huge, brick, blast furnaces constructed in 1757, close to the river beside the B4373. The Ironbridge Gorge Museums are a series of sites dotted around the area, all with their own individual character and perspective on Ironbridge's past. Consider getting a ticket for them all, but you might need a week to absorb them in full! The Ironbridge Gorge Museums include the Museum of the Gorge (the former Coalbrookdale Company Warehouse, beside The Wharfage car park at the start of Section 9), Coalbrookdale Museum of Iron, Coalport China Museum, Jackfield Tile Museum, Hay Inclined Plane and the Tar Tunnel and Blists Hill Victorian Town. The latter is great for children; an open-air museum recreating the town's industrial heyday, complete with costumed actors!

"The most extraordinary district in the world": the Ironbridge World Heritage Site

"From Coalport to Ironbridge, two miles, the river passes through the most extraordinary district in the world: the banks on each side are elevated from a height of from 3 to 400 feet, studded with ironworks, brickworks, Boat Building Establishments, Retail Stores, Inns and Houses, perhaps 150 vessels on the river, actively employed or waiting for cargoes; while hundreds and hundreds of busy mortals are assiduously engaged, melting with the heat of the roaring furnace."

Charles Hulbert, *The History and Description of the County of Salop*, 1836

Some sense of Ironbridge's industrial heritage can be gained from paddling through the Gorge, but paddlers are recommended to put aside a day or so ashore to explore and enjoy the area.

Ironbridge Gorge was primed to become the 'cradle of the Industrial Revolution' due to the raw materials available locally: wood, coal, iron ore, limestone and clay. It was however the Darby family's achievements which sparked revolutionary change. In 1708 Abraham Darby I moved from Bristol to take over the Coalbrookdale ironworks. In 1709 he pioneered smelting iron using coke (baked coal) instead of charcoal. This cheaper, faster process triggered an extraordinary expansion of activity in the gorge; by the mid-eighteenth century, iron production (literally) burned through 100,000 tonnes of coal a year, mined at Madeley and Broseley. The iron was carried by horse-drawn plateway to wharves beside the Severn and loaded onto trows for the journey downriver; a fleet of 139 boats was owned in the gorge, supplied by the shipbuilders at Bower Yard. Other major industries included the manufacture of tiles, bricks, pottery and clay pipes.

Abraham Darby II built upon his father's innovations by developing iron cylinders for Thomas Newcomen's steam engines (cheaper than the brass previously used) and in 1779, Abraham Darby III unveiled the Iron Bridge which quite literally put 'Ironbridge' on the map.

By 1873, there were 232 furnaces around Coalbrookdale. Floating amongst today's idyllic greenery, it's hard to visualise the environmental devastation wrought by all this industry, which denuded the hillsides, generated vast heaps of waste spoil and polluted the river*. Composer Charles Dibdin, visiting in 1787, was horrified; *"Coalbrookdale wants nothing but Cerberus to give you an idea of the heathen hell. The Severn may pass for the Styx ... the men and women might easily be mistaken for devils and furies"*.

* *Not to mention the effects on the climate, evident with three centuries of hindsight, of switching from charcoal (a sustainable and carbon-neutral resource) to coal (a non-renewable fossil fuel).*

📷 *Severn Valley Railway.*

© Quatford.

Section 10

Bridgnorth to Bewdley

Distance 23.1km
Start △ Severn Park, Bridgnorth SO 719 933 / WV15 5AF
Finish ⭕ Gardners Meadow, Bewdley SO 789 751 / DY12 2DU

Introduction

"... the Severn runs in a narrow valley with woody hills pressing upon the right and left, and oftentimes rolling glades of birch and bracken about its banks, and the entire distance beautifully varied with foliage and meadow."

Arthur Granville Bradley,
The Rivers and Streams of England, 1909

This might just be the finest paddle of the entire river! The Severn delves deep into a secluded wooded valley, bubbling over an endless series of easy and enjoyable rapids. The Severn Valley Railway winds alongside the river, so the peace is occasionally disturbed by the hoots and whistles of passing steam trains. As a friend put it, paddling this section for the first time; *"Seriously, this is the Midlands?"*

Launch points

Bridgnorth (Severn Park) SO 719 933 / WV15 5AF – large public park with riverside parking, on river left upstream of Bridgnorth Bridge. Large slipway and other points at which the water can be accessed.

Hampton Loade SO 747 865 / WV15 6HD – large riverside car park with slipway on river

left. Parking free for National Trust members.
Hampton SO 746 864 / WV15 6BN – small riverside parking area at end of lane, on river right.
Highley SO 750 830 / WV16 6NU – parking on river right, with permission from the Ship Inn. Limited access points to the water.
Upper Arley SO 763 802 / DY12 1RY – Upper Arley car park, on river left. Launch near the car park or at the slipway in the village centre.
Bewdley (Gardners Meadow car park) SO 789 751 / DY12 2DU – car park on river right, downstream of Bewdley Bridge. Height barrier.

Description

You will likely encounter more paddlers along the first half of this section than on any other part of the Severn, as it is heavily used by canoe hire companies. These launch from Severn Park in Bridgnorth and take out at Hampton Loade or Upper Arley.

Bridgnorth is certainly the most dramatic of the small towns arrayed along the Severn's length. Along the river right bank, Low Town is directly backed by 30-metre sandstone cliffs, atop which High Town is perched. Two High

Bridgnorth Cliff Railway.

Bridgnorth's ups and downs

"The town is a place of dignity and restful charm, despite its nearness to the Black Country, whose folk from time to time overflow into it."

Brian Waters, *Severn Stream*, 1949

Bridgnorth was founded in 1101 by Robert of Bellume, who built a castle and church atop the imposing cliffs. The town's physical geography (High Town and Low Town) is mirrored by the ups and downs it has experienced! It was besieged by Henry I and in 1322 it was burned during the 'Despenser War'. In 1646, it was bombarded by the Parliamentary Army; High Town, which Charles I declared possessed, *"The finest view in all my Kingdom"* was destroyed by fire and Bridgnorth Castle demolished into the current leaning ruin*. Georgian times were kinder to Bridgnorth; Low Town became a thriving port with three dockyards and 75 trows serving tanneries, ironworks and other industries. Victorian Bridgnorth boasted eight brothels!

To reach High Town from the Severn, select from seven separate sets of steep steps slicing through soft sandstone. Alternatively, brave the Bridgnorth Cliff Railway (a splendidly decrepit funicular service, 'Britain's oldest and steepest') or ascend the winding Cartway road past Bishop Percy's heavily, half-timbered House, which dates from c1580 and survived the Civil War fire.

* *Three times the angle of the tower at Pisa, apparently.*

Bridgnorth Bridge.

Town churches are prominent from the river; the Victorian tower of St Leonard's looms opposite Severn Park, whilst downstream of the bridge St Mary Magdalene is unmistakeable with its cupola (domed) tower, designed by Thomas Telford and completed in 1795.

Bridgnorth Rowing Club is based on the river left bank below Severn Park. No trace remains of Hazeldine's Iron Foundry, which in 1808 built *Catch Me Who Can*, the most famous of Richard Trevithick's pioneering steam locomotives. Opposite, a few traces of Bridgnorth Priory survive above the river right bank, only visible when ashore.

Bridgnorth Bridge with its 110-metre-long series of stone arches was designed by Thomas Telford. It was built in 1810 and widened in 1960, but some parts may date from the fourteenth century and there has been a bridge here since at least 1101, the oldest crossing still in place on the river. The large island immediately downstream of the bridge is The Bylet, whose name refers to the narrow and shallow river left channel, historically a fish trap or trow channel. A footbridge crosses to the island, now home to the Bylet Bowling Club! Underhill Street lines the river right bank; this was formerly the port quay for Low Town, with a waterwheel installed to pump water to High Town.

Bland, Bridgnorth Bypass Bridge briefly blips above, banishing Bridgnorth back behind. William Bliss noted, *"All the way down to Bewdley ... the scenery is wonderful."* (*The Heart of England by Waterway*, 1933) and he isn't wrong. In fact, it's hard to discern what, if anything, has changed along the river since he kayaked here; even the steam locomotives (of the Severn Valley Railway) remain present and correct. Rapids are surprisingly frequent, often marking the former sites of fish weirs, *"Here and there weirs check the natural efforts of the stream to increase its velocity"* (*Great Western Railway, The Severn Valley*, 1923).

The Severn is forced into a right bend by high sandstone cliffs on river left; this is Quatford.

"The rocky bank, which rises with grandeur almost approaching to sublimity from the Severn side, the solitary church on its eminence, and the surrounding beautiful combination of sylvan scenery, render this spot peculiarly deserving of notice."

Thomas Harral,
Picturesque Views of the Severn, 1824

Easy rapids take the paddler along the base of this long stretch of cliffs.

The five kilometres from Quatford to Hampton are enlivened by frequent, small rapids and riffles. One of the liveliest of these is channelled around an island, and shortly followed by two more back-to-back rapids at the sharp left corner where Mor Brook joins on river right. Shortly downstream, steeply wooded slopes near the river left bank mark the grounds of Dudmaston Hall, a National Trust property since 1978. Footpaths lead 500m up from the river to the landscaped Dudmaston Big Pool, but for a proper exploration of this attractive estate (including visiting the modern art galleries at the house), it is worth putting an afternoon aside and walking two kilometres upriver from the landing spot at Hampton Loade.

A curved pipe bridge (the Waterworks Bridge) connects the waterworks on river left with Chelmarsh Reservoir, uphill on river right. Just beyond, the Severn bends right between Hampton (river right) and Hampton Loade (river left). *Loade / lode*, a common placename along the river, is Old English for a ferry or wharf embarkation point. The Hampton cable ferry had been operating for 400 years when it closed in 2016, despite efforts

Quatford

Quatford's cliffs have a bit of history to them; in 895 Vikings camped on top, and in 912 'Camp Hill' was fortified by Æthelflæd, daughter of King Alfred and Lady of Mercia, against said Vikings.* Following the Norman Conquest, Earl of Shrewsbury Roger de Montgomery erected a motte-and-bailey castle to guard this crossing point. St Mary's Church was constructed after his wife had a vision of him crossing the English Channel in a storm; a priest augured that he would survive if she built a church wherever she next met him. Montgomery's son Robert abandoned Quatford and in 1101 set up base beside a new bridge to the north; Bridgnorth.

Although possibly she did this at the later site of Bridgnorth Castle.

to save it including the building of a new boat in 2004 by the Ironbridge Gorge Museum. Both Hamptons are tiny places; blink and you'll miss the landing spots! Hampton has the Unicorn Inn (with a campsite) and a small atmospheric railway station, just uphill; trains often pass one another here so it's a popular spot for steam buffs. Hampton Loade was the site of an iron forge and brass foundry, now it's pretty much just a car park (used by canoe hire operators) and the River and Rail Inn.

Below the Hamptons, the valley sides close in and steepen. One particular rapid stands out; a wave train leads river left of an island, with a small, ledge-like drop hidden on the smaller back channel.

The Highley / Alveley Footbridge is a single concrete span which, in 2006, replaced the Miner's Bridge from 1936. The coal mines served by this crossing closed in 1969 and the spoil heaps have been reclaimed and regreened; this is now the lovely Severn Valley Country Park, spanning both banks with a visitor centre and café uphill on river left.

A right bend is quickly followed by a left bend at Stanley, where the Ship Inn overlooks on river right; this pub opened in 1770, serving bargemen and miners. Uphill above is Highley Station, probably the finest of those preserved along the SVR and a regular film location. Across the road is the Engine House Visitor Centre, a great free museum exhibiting steam locomotives.

The Severn briefly delineates the Worcestershire / Shropshire boundary as it passes the confluence of sizeable Borle Brook on river

 *Below Hampton.*

Upper Arley.

Folly Point Rapids.

right. It then enters Worcestershire and also Wyre Forest, a vast (26 km²) area of natural woodland and managed forestry which envelops the river all the way to Bewdley. The only riverside village in the forest is attractive Upper Arley, where arches line the river left bank at a popular landing spot, above a slender 1971 footbridge marking the former site of a rope ferry. Arley (from *Ernley*; eagles' woodland enclave) is worth exploring, for the tearoom at least. Uphill, the site of Arley Castle now hosts Arley House and Gardens, a well-preserved, nineteenth-century, walled garden. Close by, St Peter's Church (twelfth century but now mostly Victorian) is a hefty edifice constructed from red sandstone barged downriver.

Many complete their paddle at Arley, but the wildest part of this section is still to come. Eymore Wood, the easternmost reach of Wyre Forest, descends steeply to the Severn on river left, as it flows beneath the rust-red Victoria Bridge. One of the river's more striking constructions, this was designed by Sir John Fowler and was the longest cast iron bridge ever built (61m) when it opened in 1861.

It might seem vaguely familiar as the hero hung from it in the 1978 movie *The Thirty-Nine Steps*, where it doubled for the Forth Bridge (which Fowler also built). If you are here as a steam train crosses, it's quite the sight.

After passing a long island, the Severn bends left beneath the slopes of Seckley Wood on river right. Trimpley Reservoir (which has watered Birmingham since 1968) is hidden on the far bank but your focus will be on the river ahead, as you are approaching Folly Point Rapids. These grade 2 rapids are the most notable and extensive below Jackfield (near Ironbridge, Section 9). They are harmless but great fun, consisting of a long bouncy train of waves followed shortly after by a tiny, natural, ledge drop, leading to Folly Point (a sharp right bend) itself. This is a good area to linger and play.

It's just four kilometres to your take-out in Bewdley. The arched bridge just past Folly Point is the Elan Valley Aqueduct, opened in 1904 by Edward VII. It conveys water from Mid-Wales to Birmingham, purely by gravity. The final approach to Bewdley is marked by

Dowles Railway Bridge.

Severn Valley Railway.

the tall but redundant pillars of the Dowles Railway Bridge, at the river right confluence of Dowles Brook; this opened in 1864 and was dismantled in 1966.

Bewdley's name means, 'beautiful place' and it is indeed a gorgeous little town. High quay walls topped by flood defences line the river right bank above (Severn Side North) and below (Severn Side South) Bewdley Bridge.

The river right quayside is backed by attractive Georgian buildings, the warehouses and merchant's homes of Bewdley's heyday when, as Geoffrey Boumphrey noted, it was, *"the great distributing centre on the Severn for the Midlands"* (*Down River*, 1936).

A rapid downstream of Bewdley Bridge leads to a small beach on river right with steps leading up; this is the take-out.

The Severn Valley Railway

It is possible to shuttle back to the start of Section 10 by steam train! The Severn Valley Railway is a glorious relic, a restored railway line following the Severn for much of its 26km course between Bridgnorth and Kidderminster, with a grand crossing at Victoria Bridge. The original line was opened from 1862 and linked Hartlebury with Shrewsbury, until closure following the 1963 Beeching Report. After years of campaigning and restoration work, the present service reopened in 1984. The SVR is largely staffed by volunteers who do everything from issuing tickets at the period-themed stations, to engineering and driving their fleet of nearly thirty steam locomotives. Nearly a quarter of a million visitors ride on the line annually!

Utilising the railway to run shuttle needs a bit of prior planning and thinking, but rewards the effort. The SVR stations in Bridgnorth and Bewdley are both located within walking distance of the suggested launch points, although in both cases on the opposite bank.

Bewdley's Georgian heyday

Located at the highest, easily navigable point, Bewdley boomed from exporting Wyre Forest coal and Welsh wool, with local industries including everything from snuff making and brass founding to bark peeling and tanning. Bewdley Bridge dates from 1798, three stone arches erected by Telford (a 1447 bridge was destroyed during the Wars of the Roses and a 1483 replacement was swept away in 1795 by meltwater floods). Aesthete Thomas Harral liked it: *"of elegant proportions, exhibiting a light and graceful appearance, superior even to that of Worcester"* (*Picturesque Views of the Severn*, 1824).

Bewdley was not connected to the new canal network; reputedly the townsfolk rejected, *"Brindley's stinking ditch"*. As a result, Stourport rapidly grew and Bewdley declined from major riverport to today's picturesque river crossing. Bewdley Museum is worth a visit, to learn more.

"Bewdley in its eighteenth-century elegance and lost opulence is the prettiest town along the river ... many industries made the wealth to build Bewdley's fine houses for its cap manufacturers, horn merchants and inland shipmasters, before a Quaker of the town opposed the coming of the canal, which created Stourport, leaving Bewdley to its charm."

Brian Waters in *Portraits of Rivers*, 1953

 Bewdley.

Bewdley.

Section 11

Bewdley to Holt Fleet

Distance 14.9km
Start Gardners Meadow, Bewdley SO 789 751 / DY12 2DU
Finish Holt Fleet Lock SO 823 634 / WR6 6NW

Introduction

"The Severn steals serenely on, through pastoral scenes of quiet but engaging charm. Hills of moderate height, and muffled betimes in foliage, trend upon the narrow vale, which is always one long carpet of meadow ... the Severn, unlike its famous twin the Thames, remains for all that a lonely river."

Arthur Granville Bradley,
The Rivers and Streams of England, 1909

This section follows the Severn through its final free-flowing exertions into the engineered Navigation, with two locks to negotiate. Despite the change in character, both halves are similarly attractive.

Launch points

Bewdley (Gardners Meadow car park) SO 789 751 / DY12 2DU – car park on river right, downstream of Bewdley Bridge. Height barrier.

Bewdley (Ribbesford Road) SO 789 740 / DY12 2TQ – a series of parking spots along the B4194 Ribbesford Road, on river right. These are just south of Blackstone Riverside car park, which is not riverside.

Stourport (Areley Lane) SO 806 711 / DY13 0AB – river right. Limited parking on Areley Lane, beside second right turn along Areley Lane. Carry / trolley 240m along bridleway lane to the river.

Stourport (Severn Meadows car park) SO 806 711 / DY13 8RB – series of car parks with height barriers on river left, upstream of Stourport Bridge. 90m to the water.

The Burf SO 813 678 / DY13 0RY – riverside parking area on river right, just past the Hampstall Inn. A path leads down to a pontoon, Inn customers only.

Holt Fleet Lock SO 823 634 / WR6 6NW – limited riverside parking on Holt Fleet Lane. Land/launch from pontoon on river left, 200m downstream of Holt Fleet Lock. The ramp to the pontoon has a canoe-unfriendly corner to negotiate.

Description

Paddling out of Bewdley, a series of riffles are the upward limit on the river, reachable by shallow-draught, powered boats. The uninteresting, Bewdley Bypass Bridge (1987) hefts the A456 overhead at an island, and you are back in the wilds of Worcestershire. The six kilometres to Stourport recall some of the beauty of the previous section and Brian Waters reckoned these, *"some of the fairest miles of the Severn"* (*Severn Stream*, 1949).

The first landmark is Blackstone Rock, a gnarled, sandstone cliff which rears from the water on river left. It's a pleasant spot and John Randall was, *"Highly pleased with the beauty and novelty of the scene."* (*The Tourist's guide to Bridgnorth*, 1875) despite spending a night here grounded midriver. These are the Severn's final rapids; you can be the judge of whether these mildest of ripples match up to the whirlpools of legend.

Ribbesford Woods line the river right hillside, which tops out where 124m Stagborough Hill peeks out above the trees. After this summit is passed, look out for tiny Gladder Brook which tumbles in from the hill; this is where the Severn Navigation officially commences and for the following 68km to the Gloucester and Sharpness Canal, the river is tamed by a series of five locks and weirs. Moored canal narrowboats and leisure craft line the banks down into Stourport-on-Severn; these will be a common sight from here to Gloucester, although the volume of actual traffic is invariably light.

The hermits of Blackstone Rock

"A pretty rock upon the edge of the water, cover'd with nature's beautiful canopy of oaks and many curious plants. Near the water upon the rock, liverwort grow plentifully."

William Stukeley,
Itinerarium Curiosum, 1724

Blackstone Rock possibly gets its name from lichen covering it. It's also known as the 'Spadefull' and was apparently flung by the Devil to block the course of the Severn. Until Lincomb Weir submerged the reef beside this sandstone cliff, this was a crossing point. The cliff was inhabited by cave-dwelling hermits who monitored the ford and had the remarkable duty of rescuing abandoned babies, floated downriver. These fortunate infants would be renamed 'Severn' and there genuinely are a fair few 'Severnes' recorded in local church registers! One of Blackstone Rock's legendary hermits was Sir Harry Wade, who retreated to the rock after his wife died on their wedding day. Years later, an unaware traveller confessed to murdering her and sought penance from Wade, now a holy man and unrecognisable. Wade revealed himself and the men fought to the death, both falling from Blackstone Rock and drowning in the whirlpools below.

Redstone Rock.

Stourport Bridge is the first sight of Stourport-on-Severn, a single 46m span attractively painted blue. It was built in 1870 by Thomas Vale. The first crossing here (1775) was constructed by the canal company who created the town; Stourport did not exist until the Staffordshire and Worcestershire Canal was completed in 1772. There was a single pub in 1766, by 1795 Stourport had already expanded to 250 houses and 1,300 inhabitants.

Directly past the bridge, Stourport Boat Club (founded 1876) is on the river right bank, whilst the river left bank is occupied by an amusement park; 'Treasure Island' is the most incongruous sight on the entire river. It's rather shabby and sorry-looking, a hangover from Stourport's tourist resort days. Beside this are two successive locks joining the canal to the Severn, fronted by landing pontoons.

The Angel Pub overlooks the river just past the canal locks, then Stourport's factories line the river left bank for three hundred metres to the confluence of the River Stour. The river left bank was the site of power stations and oil depots, now demolished. You've pretty much escaped Stourport, but huge caravan parks line the river right and then the river left banks over the following kilometre, followed by Stourport Marina on river left.

The glimmer of interest in Stourport's unprepossessing rear end is Redstone Rock, a sandstone cliff just after the river right caravan park. It is honeycombed with hollowed-out caves, dating back to prehistory. In the sixteenth century, the Bishop of Worcester was impressed (and appalled) by the caves, *"able to lodge 500 men and as ready to lodge thieves as true men. I would not have hermits masters of such dens"*. Travellers and ferrymen dwelled in the caves, serving the crossing which existed until Lincomb Weir was built;

"Waggons crossed by the ford, when the river was sufficiently low, until the dredging of the bed of the river up to the Stourport Locks rendered the ford impassable."

George Thompson, *Country Rambles Round Kidderminster*, 1914

The funeral cortege of Henry VII's son Prince Arthur crossed here in 1502, en route to Worcester Cathedral. When the final Stourport Bridge was built in 1870, the cave-dwelling Glover family who operated the ford received compensation. Landing to explore this remarkable site is possible, but awkward.

"From Stourport to Worcester the river is very pleasant, gentle fields and the occasional or–chards on either hand rising to hills beyond, with enough woods to give diversity. Here a knoll, there a terrace, and there a glimpse along a valley as you slip past."

Geoffrey Boumphrey, *Down River*, 1936

After the curate's egg that is Stourport-on-Severn, it's something of a surprise to discover that the second half of this section, to Holt Fleet, is strikingly attractive. **Lincomb Lock** is a case in point, backed by tall sandstone cliffs. A floating barrier warns of the first weir along the Navigation; head river left of the island to the lock. Opened in 1844, the lock was dug out from dry land at Cloth House Ford, named for the cloth-fulling mills along Titton Brook. Before the weir was built,

Lincomb Lock.

Lincomb Weir.

boats had to be hauled up the ford's shallows at high tide. The Severn really did not want to be dammed; it shifted five-tonne boulders during the weir's construction and engineers eventually sank weighted boats to stabilise their work. The lock drops over two metres and is fairly awkward to portage, with steep steps to lug your paddlecraft up. Launching below is easier, at a pontoon.

The sandstone cliffs on river left tower above the river for a kilometre from the lock, followed by a series of boat moorings before the Hampstall Inn is reached on the opposite bank. This hamlet is The Burf (*burf*; enclosure below a hill). If you land here (the pontoon

Above The Burf.

belongs to the Inn), check out the memorial for nine people who died in 1919 when the overloaded ferry capsized.

Below The Burf is a particularly lovely secluded stretch, with wooded hills reflected in the placid water. Tiny Dick Brook which joins on river right was actually made navigable in the seventeenth century; Andrew Yarranton built two flash locks to raise boats up to The Forge ironworks. The wooded crags that follow are Shrawley Wood; its lime trees were once coppiced for crates and the alders used by clogmakers who camped out in the woods. The Lenchford Inn, a large pub on river right, ends this wild interlude. The Severn bends left below wooded slopes topped by the village of Holt Heath, to reach the long island artificially created for **Holt Fleet Lock**. The river right channel is barred by a floating barrier, above a sloping weir. The lock is found towards the end of the river left channel, built at the same time and to the same dimensions as Lincomb Lock. As with Lincomb Lock, it can be a tough portage; the steep ramps serving the landing pontoon have two awkward corners to negotiate (not great if, for hypothetical example, you're carrying an open canoe, alone, in pouring rain), and it is a longish trek along the lane on river left to the launching pontoon downstream (also with corners). Much easier to pass through the lock, assuming you are there in working hours.

If you are finishing here, there is limited parking beside the second pontoon. If you are continuing to Worcester and into the Severn Vale, Telford's Holt Fleet Bridge beckons you, directly downstream ...

The Stourport Basins

It's well worth landing for a leg-stretch and exploration of the Stourport Basins, five inter-connected pools (there were originally seven). They are perched a surprising height above the Severn, with boats passing through two successive locks to access the them. The upper basins are crammed with diverse and colourful canal barges. This bustling scene is overlooked by the former Tontine Hotel and the Stourport Clock, a clock tower atop a warehouse which now houses Stourport Yacht Club. These, and other surrounding eighteenth century buildings, were constructed by the canal company. The Staffordshire and Worcestershire Canal was completed in 1772, engineered by James Brindley (who, remarkably, was barely literate). The canal is 76km in length, connecting the Severn to Birmingham and eventually the River Trent. It made Stourport (indeed, it literally *made* Stourport) into the northern terminus of navigation on the Severn; after its creation, traffic reduced on the upper river and trow channels silted up.

Stourport suffered a downturn in the nineteenth century, due to the opening of the Worcester and Birmingham Canal (1816) and then competition from railways:

"Railways have robbed the Severn and the canal of the traffic, which now passes by instead of into its commodious basins. We found the Canal Company's great commercial hotel, the Tontine ... diminished to proportions of one of the smallest inns in town."

John Randall, *The Severn Valley*, 1882

Stourport was reborn as a tourist resort! Visitors arrived to picnic and carouse beside the basins via the Kidderminster & Stourport Electric Tramway (opened 1898) and steamer boats serving Holt Fleet and Worcester. Stourport still attempts to present itself as a holiday destination (witness the rather grim 'Treasure Island'); undeniably the basins remain an attractive and engaging centrepiece to the town.

The Stourport Basins.

📷 *Upton-upon-Severn.*

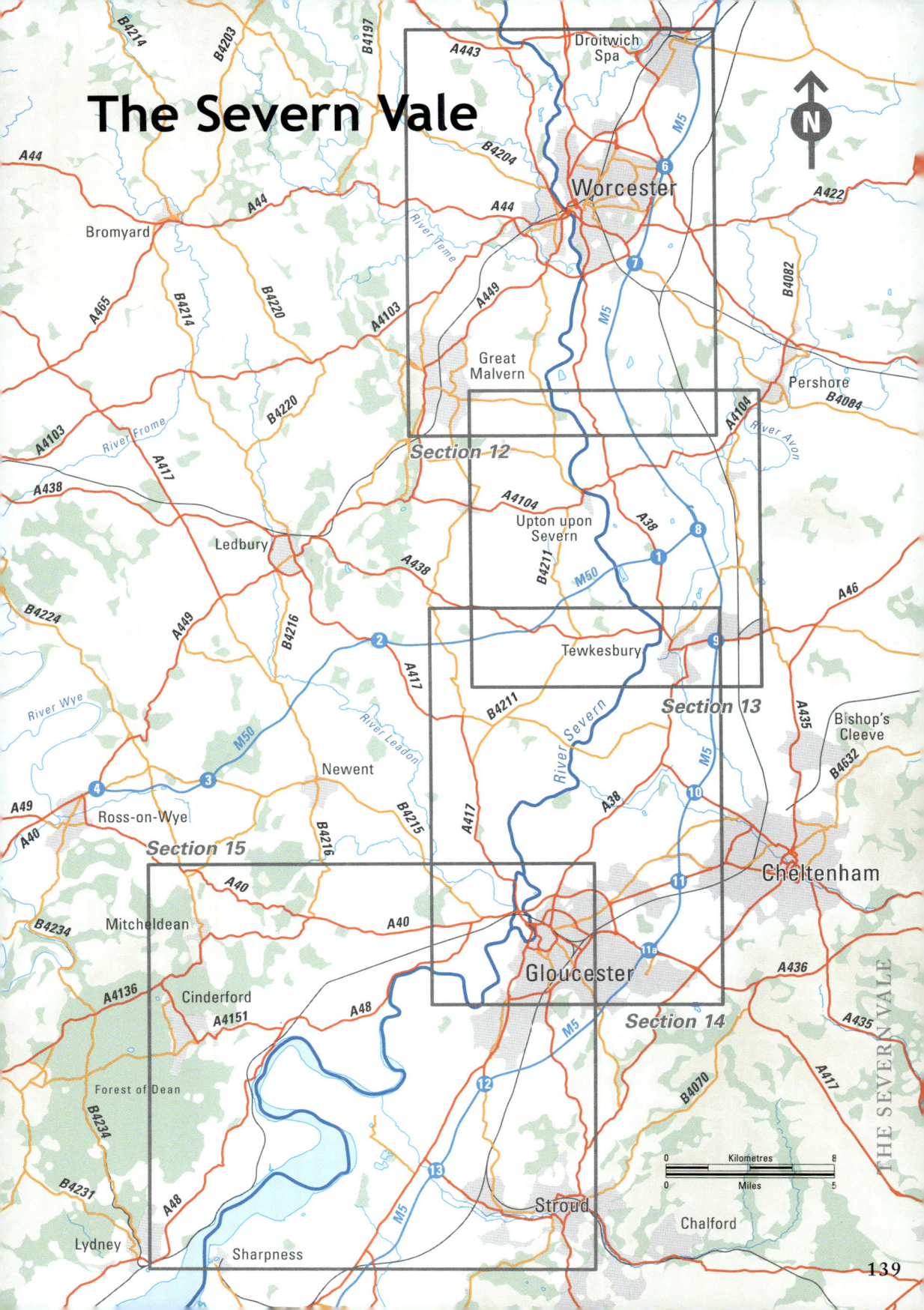

Glover's Needle.

Below Diglis Lock.

Section 12

Holt Fleet to Severn Stoke

Distance 23.4km
Start △ Holt Fleet Lock SO 823 634 / WR6 6NW
Finish ⭕ Ham Lane, Severn Stoke SO 848 444 / WR8 9JQ

Introduction

"Appreciate the beauty of the river of the vale of Severn, of the city enlivened with its lofty spires, graced with its light and elegant bridge, and backed by the sublime towers and pinnacles of its cathedral."

Francis Laird, *A Topographical and Historical Description of the county of Worcester*, 1820

The Cathedral City of Worcester, bookended by two locks, provides interest and variation in the middle of this otherwise quiet and little-frequented section of the river.

Launch points

Holt Fleet Lock SO 823 634 / WR6 6NW – limited riverside parking on Holt Fleet Lane. Land / launch from pontoon on river left, 200m downstream of Holt Fleet Lock. The ramp to the pontoon has a canoe-unfriendly corner to negotiate.

The Slip SO 835 576 / WR3 7NF – river left, public space and free parking area (AKA Northwick Lido) at the end of Old Northwick Lane. 60m to the river across a meadow. Height barrier, 250m along the lane.

Worcester Bridge.

Worcester (Waterworks Road) SO 840 564 / WR1 3EZ – river left, launch from the Pitchcroft Recreation Ground, at the end of the road. Car park with a height barrier on Waterworks Road. There is also limited parking roadside.

Worcester (Grand Stand Road) SO 844 551 / WR1 3EJ – river left, launch from Grand Stand Road which runs alongside the river. Free roadside parking.

Worcester Bridge (north) SO 846 548 / WR1 3NY – river left, Croft Road and Newport Street car parks give access to steps upstream of Worcester Bridge. It is also possible to launch downstream of the bridge near Copenhagen Street car park (height barrier).

Worcester Bridge (south) SO 846 547 / WR2 4RL – river right, steps below the bridge. Roadside parking on Hylton Road upstream of the bridge (time-limited except Sundays), public car park is directly downstream of the bridge (expensive).

Worcester (Severn Street) SO 848 542 / WR1 2NF – river left, steps where Severn Street reaches the river. Very limited roadside parking.

Worcester (Diglis Lock) SO 847 533 / WR5 3BS – river left, launch from Diglis Dock Road which runs alongside the river for 150m. Free parking roadside. Note that you can only easily launch *upstream* of the locks, where there is a pontoon.

Kempsey SO 847 491 / WR5 3JH – park roadside on Church Street outside the church, walk 100m along track to the river. Limited places to launch, may be occupied by anglers.

Pixham Ferry Lane SO 841 485 / WR2 4TQ – river right, small picnic and parking area at the end of Pixham Ferry Lane.

📷 *Holt Fleet Lock.*

Clevelode SO 835 468 / WR13 6PD – river right, very limited parking at the end of Clevelode Lane.

Severn Stoke SO 848 444 / WR8 9JQ – river left, small parking area at the end of Ham Lane.

Description

Thomas Telford's Holt Fleet Bridge carries the A4133 high above the Severn via a single, 46m cast-iron arch. It was opened in 1828 and underwent restoration in 2011. Directly below the bridge on river right is the Holt Fleet Hotel and a little further on river left is the Wharf Inn, within a caravan park. These pubs recall Holt Fleet's Edwardian glory days, when it was a popular bank holiday weekend destination; the Great Western Railway sold combined rail and steamer tickets to travel here, via Worcester.

There are no riverside settlements until Worcester, and you are unlikely to share this reach with more than a passing leisure boat or two. The banks are high and tree-covered, obscuring much of the surrounds except for the backdrop of hills. The wide river actually feels like a narrow and intimate overgrown cleft. It's worth remembering that this greenery is comparatively modern, as the shores were once kept clear to allow teams of hauliers to drag boats upstream.

You might glimpse Holt Castle on river right, after a kilometre (*Holt* is 'wood' in Old English). A formidable sandstone castle once overlooked the Severn, now recalled by a battlemented manor house and Norman St Martin's Church. After this, there are no landmarks for three kilometres until the

📷 *Bevere Lock.*

📷 *Bevere Weir.*

confluence of the River Salwarpe on river left. This sizeable stream flows from Bromsgrove and Droitwich, and the valley was utilised by engineer James Brindley to construct the Droitwich Barge Canal, which opened in 1771. This carried salt ten kilometres from Droitwich via eight locks, but fell into disuse in the early twentieth century. The canal was restored and reopened in 2010. Hawford Junction, where the canal suddenly joins the Severn via Hawford Bottom Lock, makes a surprising appearance on this quiet reach.

Bevere Island, the second largest natural island on the Severn, heralds the approach of **Bevere Lock**. The river right channel leads directly to the lock gates. The river left channel leads past a sizeable fish pass (completed 2020) and beneath a graceful, iron footbridge to the brink of the weir. It is possible, with care, to explore this side of the island and then cross beneath the island to the lock, squeezing around a barrier. *Bevere* is Old English, referring to the beaver who once thrived here. The island has also been known as The Camp; it was used as a refuge for the townsfolk of Worcester who fled here in 1041 to escape the Danes and in 1637 to escape the plague. The weir was built in 1846 on the site of the Rovin Ferry, where a bar across the river delayed traffic in low water and the tow path switched from the west to east bank. The lock itself is immaculately kept, with neatly mown lawns and flower beds. Portaging is difficult, as there is only a landing point below the lock. The Camp House Inn is on river right, shortly below the lock. The present building mostly dates from the 1930s when people came to this part of the river, known as Grimley Lido, to bathe and swim. The pub received its original license from Oliver Cromwell himself,

📷 *Camp House Inn.*

following the Battle of Worcester in 1651. This is a pleasant place to land and frequent, with peacocks pecking at your feet whilst you drink and dine.

The small beach at Northwick Lido on river left (see 'launching spots') indicates that you've reached the outskirts of Worcester. Houses crop up on river left, and when they fall back again at Pitchcroft Recreation Ground (another launch spot), houses appear on river right. A one-kilometre, near-straight leads to Worcester Bridge, passing the huge glass-fronted grandstand of Worcester Racecourse, Worcester Rowing Club (founded 1874) and also Worcester Canoe Club, all on river left. Three bridges in close succession take you to the centre of Worcester; the Sabrina Footbridge (opened in 1992, carrying the Severn Way footpath), Worcester Railway Bridge (a looming viaduct from 1860 and rebuilt 1904, carrying the former GWR Malvern and Hereford Line high above warehouses) and finally Worcester Bridge itself. The city originated here; a prehistoric settlement at the Severn's lowest fording point became a small, Roman, iron-smelting town (slag was found in the bridge foundations) which subsequently became the Saxon town of Wigorna Ceaster.

Five-arched, Worcester Bridge was designed by John Gwynne (who also designed Atcham Bridge, see Section 8) in 1781, widened in 1847 and rebuilt 1931–32. It makes for an imposing sight, surrounded by high, quay walls and backdropped by both the slender spire of Glover's Needle and the tower of Worcester Cathedral. Glover's Needle reaches 75m

📷 *Worcester.*

Worcester Cathedral

Worcester Cathedral's soaring Gothic nave abuts directly onto the Severn, with the 65m, perpendicular-style tower looming above. This is easily the most impressive human construction along the Severn's banks between Plynlimon and the sea; the flood heights carved into the Watergate and the Cathedral walls are reminders of the precarious location it occupies.

The See of Worcester was founded by Archbishop Theodore in 679. The current building originates from 1084, built for Bishop Wulfstan of Worcester. Wulfstan had personally crowned William the Conqueror in 1066; a wise career move as he became the only Saxon bishop to keep his job. Further expansions were made around 1225 and 1395. Inside, the tomb of King John (died 1216) features an effigy in Purbeck marble of the 'bad' king, the earliest likeness of an English king. Prince Arthur is also here, Henry VIII's older brother whose premature death at Ludlow robbed England of the chance to have a genuine 'King Arthur'.

towards the heavens; this eighteenth-century spire was preserved in commemoration of Worcester's glove trade, when St Andrew's Church was demolished in the 1940s.

It's possible to land in places above and below Worcester Bridge (North Quay and South Quay, respectively) but if you fancy a foray ashore, an easier spot is found 350m further on river left, at the steps of the former cathedral Watergate Ferry and directly below the cathedral itself.

Henceforth, the river right bank is green and undeveloped. The city occupies another kilometre of the river left bank; 600m past the cathedral, the Worcester and Birmingham Canal joins at Diglis Basin, surrounded by redeveloped warehouses. The canal leads 48km (via 58 locks) to Birmingham's Gas Street Basin and was connected in 1815, with two locks large enough for ocean-going ships and also a dry dock. Oil tankers came this far upstream until the late '60s. The regeneration

Worcester Cathedral.

of Diglis Dock from post-industrial wasteland into the present attractive residential district only commenced as recently as 2008.

Diglis Weir lurks on the river right side of the island below the docks, a diagonal, sloping affair measuring 150m long, with a fish pass added in 2021. Tide is sometimes recorded here (42km upstream of Maisemore Weir!); not the Bore, but river flow backed up by its pressure, an effect locally known as a 'Quarrage'. Diglis Island has seen recent redevelopment, with a visitor centre planned. **Diglis Lock** on the river left channel actually comprises two lock chambers, one small (-ish) and one large (46m long). The Severn's newest bridge (2010) is just below the lock. Diglis Bridge carries National Cycle Network Route 46 via a 66m-long span and is suspended by an unusual A-frame pylon tower. The entire site (weir, lock and island) is artificially created, opened in 1844 on a channel dug from dry land; the old channel was filled in by sinking a loaded barge.

The fields on river right were, in 1651, the site of the English Civil War's final battle, where Charles II's attempt to restore the monarchy met failure. Just a kilometre away, across the 1651 battlefield, is Powick Bridge on the River Teme, site in 1642 of the Civil War's *first* engagement. The River Teme is a sizeable tributary, 130km in length (Britain's sixteenth longest river).

The A4440 Worcester Southern Link Road Bridge is the final vestige of the city, crossing where a steeply-wooded ridge forms the river left bank. Beneath this bank, the Severn Motor Yacht Club is where rich folk, too uncultured for real yachts, moor their floating gin palaces. The remaining eight kilometres to Severn Stoke wind among attractive surrounds, with few outside intrusions. The village of Kempsey on river left only makes its presence known via riverside caravans and a brief sight of the Church of St Mary the Virgin's fifteenth century tower. The composer Elgar lived here during the 1920s, and took inspiration from the river

The Battle of Worcester 1651

The final battle of the English Civil War came nearly three years after the 1649 execution of Charles I. His son Charles II been declared king at Scone and had marched south with an army of 17,000 Scots. He headed to Worcester as it had been the first city to declare for his father and had been Charles I's headquarters, his "*Faithful City*".

"The city being nearly the whole time "in action" as it were, was more fleeced and knocked about than almost any other in England."

Arthur Granville Bradley,
The Rivers and Streams of England, 1909

Charles II utilised the Rivers Teme and Severn as defensive lines. Oliver Cromwell's Parliamentary armies hugely outnumbered the Royalists and carefully surrounded Worcester by constructing pontoon bridges to cross both rivers south of Worcester, as well as capturing Upton Bridge (see page 155) to prevent Charles from retreating. Charles led a brave attack out of Worcester's east gate, but his Scots cavalry withdrew or fled and the remains of the last Royalist army were massacred in the streets. To Cromwell's frustration, Charles escaped, eventually reaching exile on the continent.

Following the battle, radical preacher Hugh Peters sermonised that Worcester was, *"where England's sorrows began, and where they were happily ended"*.

Malvern Hills from below Kempsey.

(most obviously in his *Severn Suite*). If you can land, the church is interesting; built on Iron Age earthworks, later occupied by Romans and also a Saxon monastery sacked by the Danes. *Kempsey* is 'Kemys' Island' in Old English.

Below Kempsey, the river bends to frame the Malvern Hills directly ahead, with the 425m Worcester Beacon prominent. The river bends away to the left at the former ferry site of Pixham (a good picnic and launching spot on river right), where Simon De Montford (founder of England's first elected parliament) crossed in 1265 en route to his defeat at the Battle of Evesham. Two more left bends are characterised by steep slopes and outcrops of dark red sandstone on the river right bank. Both were ferry sites into the early twentieth century; Clevelode and *Rhydd* (Welsh for ford). A rock bar across the river below the cliffs at Cliffey Wood was a notable obstacle until it was blasted out to create the Navigation. When the Severn bends right at the end of Cliffey Wood, look out for your take-out on river left; the small parking area at the end of Ham Lane is easy to miss.

Variations

The 2.7km paddle following the River Teme upstream to Powick Bridge winds inexorably, but the five-arched bridge is lovely (with traces from the twelfth century) and is backed by an impressive mill complex. This was (unsurprisingly) the site of the Battle of Powick Bridge; see opposite.

Below Severn Stoke.

Mythe Bridge.

Section 13

Severn Stoke to Tewkesbury

Distance 16.1km
Start △ Ham Lane, Severn Stoke SO 848 444 / WR8 9JQ
Finish ⭕ Lower Lode, Tewkesbury SO 880 317 / GL20 5GL

Introduction

"I have heard it said that the Severn between Worcester and Gloucester is dull. I did not find it so. Undramatic it may be ... but a wide placid river, fringed with grey-green willows, quiet meadows and hills beyond – these do not seem dull to me."

Geoffrey Boumphrey, *Down River*, 1936
Boumphrey's experience of kayaking this stretch is precisely what you will experience today; the only changes being the M50 bridge and far fewer commercial vessels.

Launch points

Severn Stoke SO 848 444 / WR8 9JQ – river left, small parking area at the end of Ham Lane.

Hanley Castle SO 844 419 / WR8 0BS – river right, small parking area and slipway at the end of Quay Lane.

Upton-upon-Severn SO 852 407 / WR8 0HG – river right, downstream of Upton Bridge. Limited parking on Waterside. Alternatively, use Hanley Road car park, upstream of the bridge.

Lower Lode Inn SO 879 317 / GL19 4RE – river right, end of Bishop's Walk. Only for patrons or with permission.

Tewkesbury (Lower Lode) SO 880 317 / GL20 5GL – Lower Lode Lane Picnic Area, small free car park on river left at confluence of Mill Avon and River Severn.

Description

The chocolate-box, half-timbered, black and white buildings that you pass en route to the river at Severn Stoke are characteristic of this area; the Severn is now close to the River

Launching at Severn Stoke.

Avon and so-called 'Shakespeare Country'. Traffic is light on this part of the Navigation, the most likely company (other than the herons) will be rowing crews from Upton-up-on-Severn. They often train on the long straight which leads south to Severn Bank, a steep, wooded hillside on river left, forcing the river into a right bend. Severn Bank House emerges from Cliff Wood atop the slopes, a strange-looking, castellated manor house dating from 1830.

After Severn Bank falls back from the river, flood-meadows line the shores again. You might only catch glimpses of Severn End on river right, a seventeenth-century half-timbered mansion, and the only other landmark is the slipway and lane on river right, leading into the village of Hanley Castle (the castle has long gone, but a 1km walk will bring you to the earthworks).

Upton Bridge has crossed the Severn in a single span since 1940, when it replaced an 1854 bridge which had undergone various conversions into a drawbridge and then swing bridge. Upton-upon-Severn's bustling waterfront, on river right below the bridge, is

Upton Bridge.

something of a jolt after the silent river above. However, you really should take an hour or two to land and explore Worcestershire's smallest town (established 897, population: <3,000). Riverside pubs, gardens and museums, half-timbered buildings and Georgian streets; it's a lovely little place!

A steeply-stepped, flood wall (built 2011, following the 2007 flood) leads up to the Plough Inn and the King's Head pubs, alongside the unmistakeable 'Pepperpot Tower'. The tower is the remains of demolished, thirteenth-century St Peter and Paul Church, topped in 1769 by a copper-covered cupola. It's now the Upton Tourist Information & Heritage Centre, surrounded by a public garden. Other places worthy of note include the Tudor House Museum (open weekends, entry for a donation) and the White Lion, which dates from the 1550s and featured in Henry Fielding's bawdy 1749 novel *Tom Jones*. Upton was formerly, *"the great depot for cider which is brought down to its wharf and shipped to all parts of England"* (John Randall, *The Severn Valley*, 1882). Now its income derives from day tripping tourists, augmented by hosting jazz and blues festivals in the summer.

Back on the water, the entrance to Upton Marina is passed on river left before the river quickly reverts to its former quiet status. The river right shores are Upton Ham, a 60-hectare SSSI and nature reserve protecting 'Lammas meadow', flood-meadow grazed from Lammas Day (in August) to spring and then allowed to grow stock-free. Traces remain of a Victorian firing range and brick target area,

Upton-upon-Severn.

The Battle of Upton-upon-Severn

In 1651, Upton saw one of the most dramatic Civil War battles. The Severn's bridges had been severed. However, according to a contemporary account, the 300 Royalist defenders at Upton were caught off-guard because they ...

"... partook in drinking strong waters at the Inn known as The Lion where upon heavy sleep came upon them and at day dawn a forlorn hope of Ironsides crossed the plank which connected the broken bridge with the town & took possession of the church and held out until reinforced where upon the Royalists retreated to Worcester."

Eighteen hand-picked parliamentarian soldiers ('Ironsides') crossed the precarious plank and then defended the 'Pepperpot' church. A blue plaque on the waterfront commemorates Oliver Cromwell's visit the following day, to congratulate the troops in person. With the river crossing now open, Cromwell outflanked and encircled Charles II, winning the Battle of Worcester several days later.

which was also used by the Home Guard during the Second World War.

The nine kilometres to Mythe Bridge flow away from settlements and roads, with the only real landmark being the Queenshill Viaduct carrying the M50 bridge overhead, after the sharp left bend at Sandy Point. A series of large structures and wharves are distantly spaced along the river left bank, a clue to industrial activity hidden behind; Ryall Wharf is served by a fleet of barges (named after Severn fish, e.g. *Elver*) which transport aggregates three kilometres downstream to Ripple Wharf. These are the last industrial traffic on the Severn, give them a wide berth when they are on the move!

After the M50, the river leaves Worcestershire to delineate the border between Worcestershire (river right) and Gloucestershire (river left), this continues until Upper Lode, after which the river enters Gloucestershire proper.

When the river left bank steepens, you've reached The Mythe, leading down to Mythe Bridge. *Mythe* is 'river confluence' in Old English, and this hill keeps the Rivers Severn and Avon apart for a little longer. A wooded cliff lines the river, where woad has grown wild for hundreds of years. Atop the cliff are 'King John's Castle' (an ivy-covered tower which is all that remains of a 1539 manor house) and the Mythe Tut or Royal Hill (the site of a Norman motte).

Narrowboatmen used to fill their water tanks just above Mythe Bridge, believing that underwater springs made the river especially fresh here. The bridge is 84 metres long, with a single, 52-metre span of cast iron (from Coleham Foundry in Tewkesbury) and a toll house surviving on river left. When it was opened in 1826, engineer Thomas Telford boasted, "*I reckon this the most handsomest bridge which has been built under my direction*".

Upper Lode Lock.

"The reach of the river above Tewkesbury Lock, as it flows under the red wall of the Mythe cliff, was once considered by rowing men to be the second best stretch of water in England, exceeded only by Henley."

Brian Waters in *Portraits of Rivers*, 1953

The river left bank down to the confluence with the Avon is dominated by the vast, redbrick, Mythe Water Treatment Works, constructed in 1870. These were inundated by the 2007 flood, causing 150,000 homes to lose their water supply. A 3.5m wall has since been built around the site to prevent future flooding – good luck with that!

The River Avon which now joins on river left from Tewkesbury is the Old Avon, the original course of the river. An artificial, second channel, the Mill Avon, flows through the centre of Tewkesbury to join the Severn at Lower Lode (the take-out). Between the Severn and Mill Avon is the island of Severn Ham, 72 hectares of common access flood-meadow, overlooked by Tewkesbury Abbey's 45m Romanesque tower.

The final obstacle is **Upper Lode Lock** ... and it is a notable obstacle.

"We soon heard a sound of falling water, and proceeding very cautiously, we distinguished right ahead of us a mark across the river, which on our nearer approach, we found to be a weir with a heavy fall ... if we had come there at night, we should probably have gone over it."

Howard Williams, *The Diary of a Rowing Tour from Oxford to London*, 1875

Nowadays, a barrier gives warning of Upper Lode Weir. The sloping weir has a wide, sticky stopper and getting out to inspect is awkward. It is similarly tricky to portage and this isn't really recommended. Very large tides travel this far up the Severn; there was a seal swimming in the weir's stopper during our last visit! So, you need to take the river right channel and negotiate Upper Lode Lock. When this enormous construction was first opened in 1858, it was a major occasion:

"*The weir, which, with the lock, is constructed in a new channel excavated for the purpose, is 500 feet long, and is built with limestone from the neighbourhood of Chepstow ... half a dozen boats and barges sailed down the old channel, which was then closed: they then passed twice in and out of the lock. Firing of batteries and loud cheers from the assembled multitudes accompanied the opening ceremony.*"

Illustrated London News, 1858

The lock is almost impossible to portage, due to very high banks. The lock-keeper (extremely helpful, in our experience) will give you directions as to how and when to enter the lock chamber. The lock needs a full half hour to drain! Howard Williams recorded, *"I had never been in such an enormous lock before; the walls were quite 30 feet high, and all we had to do was keep our sculls in the water, and steady the boat."* (*The Diary of a Rowing Tour from Oxford to London*, 1875). The lock is now even larger than Williams experienced; the previous two chambers have been combined into a single, 92m-long amphitheatre, up to 24m wide. Sitting in a tiny paddlecraft at the heart

Lower Lode.

of this utterly vast construction, engineered for ocean-going steam tugs and barges, feels at once awe-inspiring and rather silly.

Below Upper Lode Lock, you might catch a glimpse back upstream of Tewkesbury Abbey and Bredon Hill, the sprawling Cotswold outlier which dominates the lower Avon valley. It's just a kilometre to the take-out at Lower Lode; this is located where the Mill Avon joins the Severn, almost inconspicuously. You won't miss the spot however, as it is clearly marked by the Lower Lode Inn (and campsite) on river right.

Variations

The Mill Avon offers a really engaging alternative finish to this trip, right through Tewkesbury's historic centre. It's also possible to use this to finish your trip within Tewkesbury, avoiding Upper Lode Lock. Follow the Old Avon 400m upstream to Avon Lock and portage around this to join the Mill Avon. The Mill Avon and Tewkesbury are fully described in the author's guidebook *Paddle Shakespeare's Avon*.

Approaching Maisemore Bridge

Below Lower Lode.

Section 14

Tewkesbury to Gloucester

Distance 15.4km / 19km
Start △ Lower Lode, Tewkesbury SO 880 317 / GL20 5GL
Finish ○ Maisemore Bridge SO 816 211 / GL2 8ES
○ Castle Meads car park, Gloucester SO 823 182 / GL1 2NH

Introduction

This final, (almost), non-tidal stretch of the Severn maintains the attractive solitude that has characterised the river since Worcester. There are some engaging medieval sites along the banks, and you have the option of linking up Tewkesbury and Gloucester Cathedrals by following the Eastern Channel right into Gloucester's historic centre.

Launch points

Tewkesbury (Lower Lode) SO 880 317 / GL20 5GL – Lower Lode Lane Picnic Area, small, free car park on river left at confluence of Mill Avon and River Severn.

Lower Lode Inn SO 879 317 / GL19 4RE – river right, end of Bishop's Walk. Only for patrons or with permission.

Deerhurst SO 867 299 / GL19 4BX – river left. Small parking area at the end of Deerhurst Lane, opposite Odda's Chapel. Carry or trolley 150m along a wide public footpath to a beach.

Yew Tree Inn SO 865 297 / GL19 4EQ – river right, end of Stock Lane. Pontoons at a riverside pub, customers only.

Below Haw Bridge.

Haw Bridge SO 844 278 / GL19 4HJ – river right, above and below the bridge. Park roadside, there are pontoons below the bridge. If the Haw Bridge Inn reopens check with them first.

Red Lion SO 847 258 / GL2 9LW – river left. Riverside parking and beer garden, across the road from the pub. Launch, with permission, from the beach at the downstream end of the garden.

Ashleworth Quay SO 818 250 / GL19 4HZ – river right, small parking area at the end of Quay Lane. Launch at the dilapidated quay, tricky.

Maisemore Bridge SO 816 211 / GL2 8ES – river right, upstream of bridge. Follow a rough path between coal bunkers, behind houses to a fishing platform. Awkward to land or launch due to steep banks, metalwork and masonry in the water. Park roadside in Maisemore, e.g. on Bridge Farm.

Gloucester (Docks) SO 827 186 / GL1 2JN – river left, steep steps from the East Channel onto The Quay: tricky! Nearest parking is North Warehouse car park, 150m south along the road. Only recommended for those transferring to the Docks and Gloucester and Sharpness Canal.

Gloucester (Castle Meads car park) SO 823 182 / GL1 2NH – river right on East Channel of River Severn, beneath A430 bridge. Egress up muddy banks (awkward) and carry / trolley 50m to car park.

Haw Bridge.

Description

Rowing through here, Howard Williams was uncharacteristically jaded;

"The Severn at this part, and in fact, all the way to Gloucester is very wide, and the stream very sluggish. There is no scenery to speak of; the surrounding country is very flat, and on each side of the river there are high banks, so that we could really see nothing."

The Diary of the Rowing Tour from Oxford to London, 1875

Williams must have been having an off day, because he was wrong, wrong, wrong. The hills do come close at times, there is plenty of interest (if you know what to look for) and trees line the banks, draping into the steadily-flowing water: this is a lovely secluded paddle. Incidentally, be aware that very high spring tides have reached as far upstream as Tewkesbury, having over-topped Maisemore Weir.

The first highlight comes just 2.3km from the start. After passing the stone tower of St Mary's Church on river left, land at the muddy beach at SO 867 299 and walk 150m along a footpath to explore the tiny hamlet of Deerhurst, where two of the most complete Early Medieval buildings in England survive.

The only landmarks before Haw Bridge are moorings (a sunken barge) at the Yew Tree Inn on river right, and the Coal House Inn on river left, where there is a caravan park. Haw Bridge itself appears suddenly around a corner; an austere concrete affair built in 1961. It filled the vacancy left in 1865 when an 1825 bridge was accidentally demolished by the tanker *MV Darleydale*

The Cliff.

Odda's Chapel.

(killing the skipper). There are disused pubs on both sides of the B4213 on river right; the Haw Bridge Inn is closed at time of writing.

When the river enters a long right bend, look for a lock gate on river left. Coombe Hill Canal was opened in 1796 to bring coal to Cheltenham, but only half the distance was completed (4.5km). It was abandoned after flood damage in 1876. The waterway has now been restored as a Gloucestershire Wildlife Trust reserve.

Shortly after, the Red Lion Inn and adjoining campsite on river left are backdropped by Wainlode Hill and The Cliff. As the name suggests, The Cliff is a sheer cliff, eroded from soft Keuper marl. Two tall posts in mid-river direct large vessels to river right. The posts mark where a number of barges have been sunk to prevent further erosion; the barges are not normally visible. The Cliff gives way to the wooded slopes of Norton and Sandhurst Hills, rising 80m from the water (decent viewpoints, should you stretch your legs ashore).

The river right bank is Ashleworth Ham, a 105-hectare Gloucestershire Wildlife Trust reserve of flood-meadows and wetlands.

Exploring Deerhurst

The first building you reach from the river is Odda's Chapel. This was built in 1056 for Earl Odda, to pray for the soul of his recently-deceased brother Aelfric. The simple but hefty building was hidden in plain sight until 1865, when it was rediscovered incorporated into a sixteenth-century half-timbered farmhouse. Just along the lane is St Mary's Church, dating from around 700AD; people have worshipped here continually for 1,300 years! A close look inside and outside will reveal plenty of truly ancient Early Medieval stonework.

In 1016, Deerhurst was witness to the last Viking conquest of England*. Following King Edmund's defeat in battle by Cnut the Great, the two met on an island at Deerhurst and Edmund ceded the north to the Viking. Edmund was dead within a month, at which point Cnut claimed all of England.

Unless you count 1066; William the Conqueror and his Normans ('Northmen') were of course Viking descendants.

📷 *Ashleworth Quay.*

📷 *Ashleworth Tithe Barn.*

Huge numbers of wildfowl are found here when the waters rise in winter (grebes, pintail, teal and widgeon), whilst in summer reed buntings, sedge warblers and snipe hide their nests among the reeds and tall grass.

Ashleworth Quay follows on river right, marked by a church steeple and a ramshackle landing stage on the outside of a sharp left bend. This was the site of a horse ferry, where the towpath changed banks to avoid The Cliff. The ferry possibly operated since Roman times, based on remains found here. The Boat Inn is a lovely pub, in buildings dating from the fifteenth century. It unfortunately closed after flooding in 2020 and may not reopen.

The 3.5km following Ashleworth veers south, called the Long Reach. It ends abruptly at Upper Parting, where the Severn splits into two. The West Channel bends sharply to the right; this is larger, but only became the main channel in the late fifteenth century when a flood broke through a levee into a backwater. The smaller East Channel, which is the Navigation channel, continues south into Gloucester. Between the two channels is 3.4km-long Alney Island, consisting of huge flood-meadows (Maisemore Ham, Town Ham, Port Ham, Oxlease and Castle Meads). The island is largely undeveloped, although somebody thought it a good idea to site Castle Meads electricity sub-station, serving a third of a million people, on the island; in the 2007 floods, there was an epic and barely-successful battle to divert waters around the sub-station.

Ashleworth Tithe Barn

At Ashleworth, definitely make the effort to walk 150m up Quay Lane to explore impressive Ashleworth Tithe Barn, built in 1481 alongside a church and manor house. Tithe Barns were enormous warehouses (this one measuring 38m x 8m) used to store 'tithes', 10% of everyone's produce which had to be surrendered to the Church. The three monastic vows were 'poverty, chastity, obedience'; it's not clear how collecting tithes related to the first vow.

The West Channel

Paddling the West Channel brings you to the take-out above Maisemore Bridge in just 800m ... with the notable obstacle of Maisemore Weir to negotiate en route (Maisemore is Welsh in origin; *maes mawr*, great field). The weir is a huge, multi-levelled structure with potential routes for experienced, white-water paddlers in very low water conditions, however with limited opportunity to inspect or protect and the added complication that the downstream water level changes with the tide ... most will sensibly portage. The remains of Maisemore Lock (defunct since the Gloucester and Sharpness Canal was opened) are preserved on the river left bank, which is private land. To portage, land a safe distance above the weir on river right and follow the footpath along the bank, through a gate. A small path leads from the footpath down steps to the weir pool: if you find yourself atop a cliff looking back at the weir, you have overshot the path and need to backtrack a bit.

Back on the water, it's just a few paddle strokes down to your egress point, on river right upstream of Maisemore Bridge.

Note that you don't want to be on this short final stretch of river during the relatively rare moments when the Severn Bore surges up here! Check online that no Bore is forecast.

The East Channel

Paddling the East Channel into Gloucester makes for a longer trip (3.6km longer, to be precise). The channel is narrow and fairly

Maisemore Weir.

The entrance to Gloucester Docks.

fast-flowing, hemmed in between high, tree-lined banks alongside Alney Island. There are few clues as to the approach of the city, until you pass beneath a series of bridges in quick succession; the A44 Walham Bridge, Black Bridge (a railway bridge) and the three adjacent A417 Westgate Bridges (the middle one is a footbridge).

Be awake now, as things happen quickly! After rounding a right bend, you see the high and imposing gates of Gloucester Lock directly ahead; the lock opened in 1812 (it was reopened in 2019 after a £300,000 repair), replacing a previous staircase of locks. This is the entrance to Gloucester Docks and the Gloucester and Sharpness Canal. If you intend to visit or transfer to these (paddlers are not allowed in the lock), you must immediately egress using the steps on river left upstream of the lock gate; there are no other ways off the water on this bank. To make things more awkward, there may be vessels moored along this quay wall, waiting to enter the lock. If you are planning to egress above Gloucester Lock, call ahead and notify the lock-keeper (01452 310832 or VHF channel 74).

The East Channel.

The Port of Gloucester

The UK's most inland port originated c47AD as a Roman settlement, located around the then-lowest fording point on the river. In 97AD it became Colonia Nervia Glevensium, a colony for retired legionaries. Gloucester's awe-inspiring cathedral, overlooking the East Channel, had its origins in 679 as St Peter's Abbey. The town received a charter from Henry II in 1155, which included freedom of passage on the Severn. Elizabeth I awarded Gloucester its port status (presumably no one showed her a map) in 1580. The 'port' of Gloucester remained fairly difficult to access from the sea until the completion of the Gloucester and Sharpness Canal in 1827.

Gloucester's docks have been gentrified in recent times, with warehouses renovated and cafes and shops lining the basins. It is worth visiting the National Waterways Museum which occupies a former warehouse, and the Gloucester Life Museum which has displays on the Severn and is close to the cathedral.

Gloucester Docks.

Otherwise, continue past the lock gates beneath Castle Meads Footbridge, looking out for convenient spots to land along the river right bank. The banks are overgrown and muddy, this will need care. The last (and probably easiest) spot is beneath the A430 Castle Meads Bridge. Before heading upstream to the car park, consider exploring the footpath downstream to where tall nettles hide the remains of now-dry Llanthony Lock.

Warning

Directly downstream of Castle Meads Bridge, the Severn flows for just 150m, beneath Llanthony River Bridge (a derelict railway bridge) and Llanthony Lock Footbridge (closed to the public), before reaching Llanthony Weir. It's **impossible to inspect* or portage** the weir, so approaching this really is to be avoided. The weir is cluttered with wood and other flood debris and is also overtopped by large 'spring' tides (over 7.2m in height); the author knows of a group who were caught out here after previously having 'inspected' the river using Google Maps, which shows high tide conditions with no sign of Llanthony Weir ...

From the weir it is just a kilometre to Lower Parting, where the East and West Channels converge; see Section 15.

---

*The author viewed the weir after three separate failed nettle-battling attempts, approaching from different directions.

Newnham

Approaching the Noose.

Section 15

Gloucester to Sharpness

Distance 46.7km
Start △ Maisemore Bridge SO 816 211 / GL2 8ES
Finish ◯ Sharpness Lifeboat Station SO 667 029 / GL13 9UB

Introduction

"Severn tide runs through an enchanted land where the pear trees grow to giant size, becoming a mass of white in April when they gleam against the blueness of the hills of Malvern, the greenery of Cotswold and the dark blue bushland of the Forest of Dean."

Brian Waters in *Portraits of Rivers*, 1953
These final reaches of the Severn wind tortuously as it morphs from freshwater river to saltwater expanse. This is a very serious and challenging trip requiring careful thought and pre-planning, but the reward is access to a remarkable wild and open landscape, spiced up with a fair amount of excitement.

Launch points

Maisemore Bridge SO 816 211 / GL2 8ES – river right, upstream of bridge. Follow a rough path between coal bunkers, behind houses to a fishing platform. Awkward to land or launch due to steep banks and masonry in the water. Park roadside in Maisemore, e.g. on Bridge Farm.

Strand Lane SO 715 132 / GL14 1PG – river right. Follow Strand Lane to the river wall. Parking area for several vehicles, otherwise park back up the lane. Muddy.

Newnham SO 693 120 / GL14 1BH – river right. Newnham car park beside the A48, waterside. Muddy.

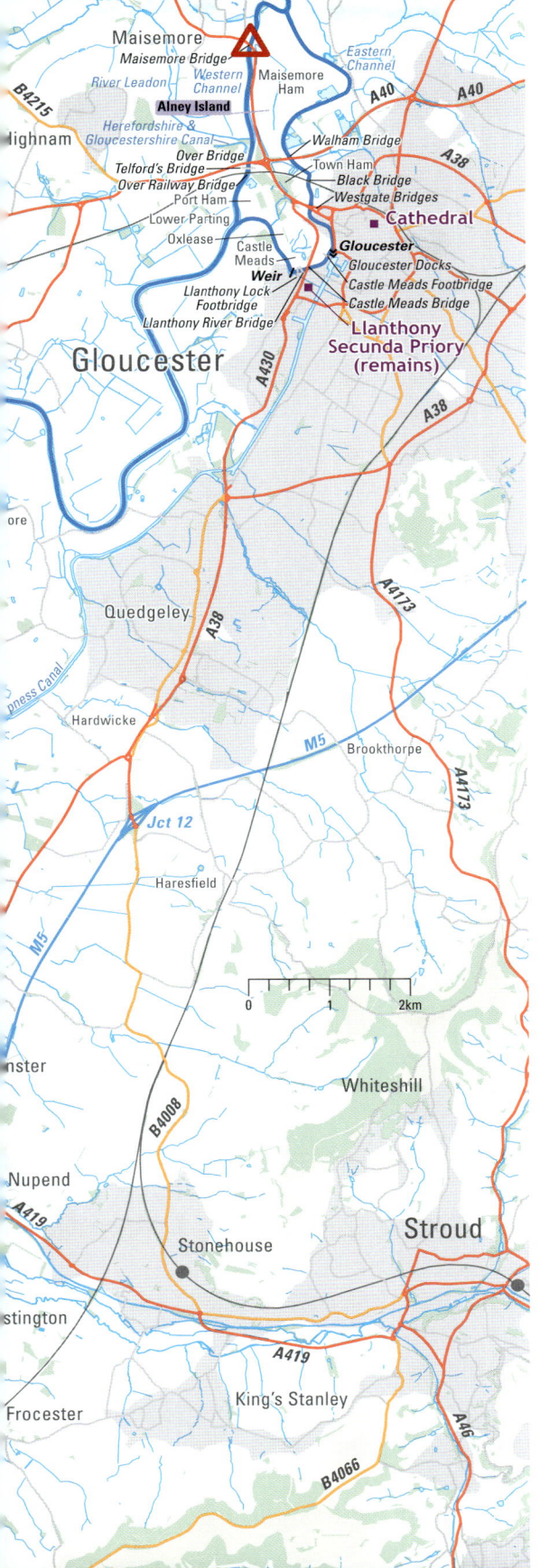

Sharpness Lifeboat Station SO 667 029 / GL13 9UB – river left. Land at the slipway below SARA Sharpness Lifeboat Station and carefully carry up the muddy slipway to the Gloucester Ship Canal. Carry (or ideally, trolley!) 350m along a track to Purton car park SO 671 028/ GL13 9UN. The slipway is privately owned, use discretion and certainly don't block access. If in use, you may have to continue **950m** downstream and attempt egress just past the dock entrance: very muddy and very unappealing.

Planning

"The river can, of course, be navigated beyond Gloucester, but the stretch to the mouth of the river is in tidal water, with shifting sands and channels, and, of course, the famous "bore." If attempted at all, it should only be tackled by really expert canoeists."

Alec R. Ellis, *The Book of Canoeing*, 1935
You don't have to be, *"really expert"*, but you certainly need to be well informed and plan carefully. This long outing can be broken down into shorter paddles of 26km and 20.7km, by using the muddy launch point at Strand Lane (or Newnham, 2.5km further downstream); this approach also offers the possibility of avoiding the more exposed and challenging second half. However, if you have the capability to tackle the whole trip, do it! The distance falls away easily due to strong tidal flows. There is upwards of eight hours between high water (HW) and low water (LW) at Sharpness; even launching two hours after

Launching at Maisemore Bridge.

HW Sharpness (see below) should give you sufficient time to cover the distance.

Tide times for Sharpness can be found online. It is recommended to only attempt this at 'neap' tidal flows, when the range between HW and LW is smallest. These conditions are encountered just over a week after full moons and new moons. At 'spring' tides, the range between HW and LW is genuinely extreme (14.8m+ at Sharpness, the third highest in the world after Canada's Bay of Fundy and Ungava Bay) and the infamous Severn Bore is generated on the flood tide. Although you will be paddling on the ebb tide (hence, hopefully avoiding the Bore), spring tide flows will generate some pretty fearsome rough water conditions in the latter part of your trip; even paddling at neap tide flows involves a fair amount of white-water paddling technique.

You will need to launch from Maisemore just as the tide begins to ebb (fall) at the bridge. It's not easy to predict when this will happen! At spring tides, the tide rises incredibly quickly at Sharpness (as little as three hours between low and high tide) and arrives spectacularly at Maisemore as the Bore, overtopping the weir upstream. It then surges higher again for a further hour or so (the 'big muddy') before rapidly switching direction to ebb strongly (carrying trees and other debris swept up by the Bore). As noted, these conditions can't be recommended. At neap tides, there is no Bore and the water rises gradually. Tidal effect might even be hard to discern, as far upstream as Maisemore; the switch in direction to the ebb flow is mild and unspectacular. Watch from Maisemore Bridge and assume that this will happen around two hours after high water at Sharpness, with plenty of variation (caused by freshwater river flow, air pressure and other factors).

Other factors to consider include wind and mud. Avoid strong winds, which generate 'wind-over-tide' conditions; the tidal flows get whipped up into steep and breaking waves. As you progress down the estuary, areas of silt and mud become exposed along the banks, making it hard or even dangerous to leave the river. For this reason, you should familiarise yourself with the various take-out options before paddling.

If you wish to notify Sharpness Dock of your approach, call 01453 511968 or 'Sharpness Radio' on VHF Channel 13. VHF reception is poor along the river.

Gloucester Harbour Trustees publish a useful 'Small Craft Guidance' booklet which can be downloaded from their website.

Over Bridge.

Description

After all the fuss of planning and preparation, the river at Maisemore will hopefully be anticlimactically sedate! Leaving Maisemore Bridge (1956) behind, the Severn follows a course directly south, lined by trees and looking pretty much as it has done all the way from Worcester, with the single difference of a muddy, inter-tidal zone lining the shores.

After 1.5km the River Leadon trickles in on river right; directly below is the spot where the Herefordshire and Gloucestershire Canal joined. This was built in two phases (1798 and 1845), had a fairly short life and closed in 1881 due to railway competition. The canal basin at Over has been restored, and the lock into the Severn may eventually be restored. This spot is over-shadowed by the three successive Over Bridges that follow; the New Over Bridge (1974) carrying the A40, Over Bridge (1830) and Over Railway Bridge (1957). It's the now-disused, middle Over Bridge which is the interesting one, indeed it's maintained by English Heritage. Thomas Telford constructed it utilising the longest masonry span in England, where Roman Ermine Street crossed. When the wooden 'centring' supports were removed, the centre of the arch unexpectedly subsided by 25cm, an awkward moment for Telford. The bridge still stands, although its eroding sandstone is causing concern.

The East Channel joins from river left at Lower Parting. In truth, there isn't much to say about the following sixteen kilometres, as the river continues in similar vein; high banks,

Stonebench Bend.

Garden Cliff.

occasional houses, wide vistas across the flood plain to the hills of the Forest of Dean and the Cotswolds. At Stonebench where the Gloucester and Sharpness Canal is just 200m away, an entire ship sits permanently berthed ashore, now some lucky fellow's home. Stonebench, and Minsterworth on river right, are popular Bore-watching spots, the latter identifiable by the turreted stone tower of its church, followed by the Severn Bore Inn.

The first notable change in the river comes when the shores fall back at Longney Sands; the river follows a channel through 600m-wide mud and sand flats, the haunt of wading birds in winter. You are hemmed in by sandbanks and the river can be deceptive; you'll strain your eyes checking that you have picked the correct, deep channel. This foretaste of things to come only lasts for 1.5km, before the river narrows again at Longney Crib.

Upper Framilode on river left is another village identified by a church tower, this time with a pointed roof on top. Located at the confluence of the River Frome, this was formerly a port for the Stroudwater Navigation.

The following thirteen kilometres loop around the Arlingham Peninsula, which finishes at Hock Cliff, less than two kilometres from Framilode! The river gradually widens to around 600m, always with a distinct channel to locate and follow. Red-green Garden Cliff on river right is a popular fossil-hunting spot, where the river is eroding late Triassic mudstones. The beach beyond the cliffs at Strand is a possible take-out. Around a left bend, Newnham makes for a dramatic sight. Arrayed around The Nab cliff, the village's Victorian houses and prominent church appear somehow continental and distinctly un-English. The village grew around a ferry and ford, which existed

Longney Sands.

from at least 1238 and was possibly used by the Romans; on the far river left bank, the crossing point is recalled by the remote Old Passage Inn. Just past Newnham, Collow Pill is an arresting boatyard / ship's graveyard, with an array of large vessels hauled up on the mud. The lightship arrived in 2015; it was launched in 1953 and mostly used off the Gower Peninsula, before spending several years as a floating café in Cardiff Bay.

Hock Cliff (Jurassic limestone, another fossil-hunting site) on river left is fronted by shallow reefs. It marks the end of the Arlingham Peninsula and the point at which the Severn balloons to two kilometres wide. The Noose (passed along the river left bank) and then Frampton Sand (passed along the river right bank) are a five-kilometre expanse of

The Noose.

sand. Paddlers receive conflicting signals; on the one hand, the open landscape, wide horizons and lack of human influence simply wow, it's easy to drift along imagining that you are in the Yukon, not Gloucestershire. On the other hand, the paddleable channel is actually relatively narrow, intimate and indeed lively, focusing your attention on the task at hand.

Collow Pill.

Frampton Sand.

The current rips along past high banks of sand. Whatever conditions you encounter, you are at this point pretty much committed to them. The author experienced continuous, bouncy waves and boily, white water through the Noose and Frampton Sand, conditions which ramped up further, in the narrower, final five kilometres to Sharpness. This was exhilarating and indeed great fun, but would be a catastrophic environment in which to practice your swimming skills ... and this was just neap flows! Open canoes will likely fill up and swamp.

The excitement of the final approaches to Sharpness mean that you'll probably pass unaware of Slimbridge Wetland Centre, an 800-hectare nature reserve located to river left of Middle Point, where the Severn turns to pass between the Noose and Frampton Sands. Likewise, you will likely be too preoccupied to take note of Purton Ships' Graveyard along the river left shore, a remarkable site where 86 ships and barges were grounded between 1909 and 1965 to protect the Gloucester and Sharpness Canal from being breached. Both of these spots are most definitely worth visiting from land, after your paddle.

Purton Ships' Graveyard.

◻ *Approaching Sharpness.*

The approach to Sharpness follows the rocky river right shore, backed by a busy rail line. Sharpness is impossible to mistake, being marked out by a tall wind turbine. It could however potentially be missed! Make sure that you cross the tidal current in good time to land at the slipway. This is located at Sharpness Point, where the high walls of Old Sharpness Docks finish. The new (working) docks are 850m downstream, and somewhat harder / muddier to land below.

It is a further 24km from Sharpness to the Severn's 'official' end. However, although the Severn is possibly still a 'river' when it reaches Sharpness, beyond this point is indisputably the sea.

Variations

The entirety of Section 15 can be safely bypassed using the Gloucester and Sharpness Canal. As the name implies, this connects Gloucester Docks with Sharpness Docks. The distance by canal is much shorter (26.5km) and a number of adventurers paddling around Wales or between Lands End and John O'Groats have made use of this route. The canal can of course be used as a return route after paddling Section 15.

From Sharpness, you can see the two Severn Bridges spanning the Severn Estuary downstream. The M48 Severn Road Bridge was opened in 1966, crossing in a 988m-span from Aust Rock to Beachley. Beyond this is

The Severn Bridges from Sharpness.

the 5km-long, M4 Second Severn Crossing, opened in 1996; an astonishing bit of engineering, given that its pillars rise from some of the strongest and fastest tidal waters on earth. The Severn's 'official' end is a line between Severn Beach in Gloucestershire and Sudbrook in Monmouthshire, which crosses the Second Severn Crossing at around 352km from the source, by the author's reckoning (Wikipedia reckon 354km, but I'm guessing that they haven't actually paddled it). The notably committing and dangerous voyage passing beneath the Severn Bridges (including the world's third highest tidal range and only one reliable landing spot in over 40km) is beyond the scope of this book, and is described in the author's guidebook *South West Sea Kayaking*.

The Severn Railway Bridge Disaster

From 1879 the Severn Railway Bridge, a 1269m 22-span rail viaduct, crossed from Sharpness Docks to Lydney Docks. Before the Severn Road Bridge was opened (1966), this was the lowest crossing of the Severn. In 1960, two tanker barges carrying oil overshot Sharpness in fog. They collided with one another and also the bridge (which carried a gas main), collapsing two bridge spans. The result was an almighty explosion in which five died; the heat actually fused the ships to the bridge. The Severn Railway Bridge was not fully demolished until 1970 and the tankers are still visible at low water.

Paddling the Gloucester and Sharpness Canal

The canal is a monster! Built to accommodate ships up to 73m long and 550 tonnes in weight, it is 26m wide and 5.5m deep; when opened, it was the widest and deepest in the world. It is very popular with paddlers, being much safer than the estuary and easy to access from numerous spots. It is surrounded by some attractive scenery, as well as historic buildings such as warehouses, inns and ornate bridge keepers' houses. There are no locks, the only physical obstacles encountered are swing bridges. There is little traffic, you just have to steer clear of the occasional leisure craft. Be careful around Sharpness Docks however, this working port handles commercial vessels up to 6,500 tonnes.

It was constructed to bypass the wriggly parts of the estuary, shortening the c48km route to 26.5km. A 1793 Act of Parliament sparked the canal's construction, but long delays were caused by financial problems and the Napoleonic War. In 1817, Thomas Telford was brought in as an engineering consultant and the government invested in the project on the condition that Napoleonic veterans were employed. Telford managed to get it finished in 1827 at a total cost of £440,000.

A Canal & River Trust license is required to paddle on the canal.

Gloucester and Sharpness Canal.

The Severn Bore at The Severn Bore Inn.

The Severn Bore

"And on the angry front the curled foam doth bring
The billows gainst the flanks when fiercely it doth fling;
Hurls up the slimy ooze, and makes the scaly brood
Leap madding to the land affrighted from the flood,
O'erturns the toiling barge."

Michael Drayton, *Poly-Olbion*, 1612

The Severn Bore is a remarkable natural phenomenon, a wall of tidal water which surges *up* the river with unstoppable force and daunting speed. Bore-watching, an activity in its own right, is a great way to enjoy this spectacle from a safe distance. Vicarious thrills will not satisfy everyone, however; expert paddlers will want to attempt surfing the wave in their paddlecraft ...

About the Bore

The Severn Bore takes its name from the Old English *bara* (wave). It is caused by the rising tide being funnelled up the Bristol Channel and then the Severn Estuary into shallower water, boosted by the third highest tidal range in the world. The Bore first becomes visible at the narrowing of the Severn between Fretherne and Awre, upstream of the Noose sand flats. Initially a smooth rolling wave, it steepens and breaks as the river narrows further. Eventually, this upstream-travelling slab of water is further compressed to form a succession of steep breaking waves, one following the other. The Bore travels upriver at 13 to 21kph, quite literally smashing its way past obstacles such as riverbanks and bends; an alarming sight to watch, let alone surf! The front wave is most commonly up to 1.3m high, but can exceptionally reach two metres in height. The largest recorded wave was 2.8m(!), seen at Stonebench in 1966. The Bore takes a little over two hours to cover the 40km from Awre to Gloucester. When it reaches Alney Island it splits, to collide with Maisemore and Llanthony Weirs on the West and East Channels, respectively. The surge overtops both weirs (and occasionally also Upper Lode Weir at Tewkesbury, a further 16km upstream) but the wave has spent its

181

energy and is now diminished. A ninth-century Welsh monk described the Bore parting at the Noose, or possibly Alney Island:

"Another wonder is the Dau ri Hafren, that is the two kings of the Severn. When the sea fills the estuary of the Severn in the flood tide, two heaped up wave crests are built up separately and fight each other in the fashion of rams ..."

Nennius, *Historia Brittonum*, 828

Nennius noted that the Bore has consistently formed, *"... from the beginning of the World until the present day"*. The reason for this is of course the effect of the moon in generating tides. The Bore forms on spring tides of nine metres or greater at Avonmouth. Spring tides are those with the highest range between high and low water. They are caused by the moon and sun being aligned with the earth for maximum gravitational pull and occur for several days after full or new moons. The largest spring tides occur around the Spring and Autumn Equinoxes in March and September, when the sun is directly above the equator. Bores occur on about 130 days a year, twice daily of course. The Environment Agency publish Bore predictions rated from 1* to 5*; the photos here show three-star Bores. A five-star Bore is a rare event as the size wanes and waxes on a nine-year cosmic cycle; for example, none were predicted larger than three stars in 2021 and 2022, and just a single (night-time) five-star bore was predicted for 2023.

The size of the Bore is also affected by a number of environmental factors. Following winds (from the south-west) increase its size and speed, and headwinds have the opposite effect. High river flows (and also really low flows!) also decrease the size and speed of the wave, although these have the opposite effect in the lower estuary.

Viewing the Bore

Various spots allow decent public access to view the Bore. The classic Bore-watching spots are outlined here, in upstream order:

Newnham SO 693 120 / GL14 1BH – Newnham car park on the river right bank (also the White Hart Inn, 1km upstream) allows folk to see the bore for the longest period of time.

The Severn Bore Inn SO 754 153 / GL2 8JX – This pub on the river right bank, beside the A48 south-west of Minsterworth, has a viewing platform for Bore-watching customers. For early tides, they lay on breakfast – perfect!

Stonebench SO 795 148 / GL2 3NP – Elmore Lane West gives access to the footpath along the river left bank.

Over Bridge SO 816 195 / GL2 8BZ – Follow the pedestrian underpass from Horseshoe Drive to the bridge.

Awaiting the Bore at The Severn Bore Inn.

📷 *The Severn Bore.*

All of these spots can suffer from parking issues, which test the patience of locals. Do your best to be considerate and minimise any disruption caused.

Surfing the Bore

"A fine bore comes roaring up the river with the speed of a horse at canter, followed by the torrent of the tide, and only a boat facing head on can ride the wave."

Brian Waters in *Portraits of Rivers*, 1953
Perhaps Second World War veteran 'Mad Jack' Churchill* was inspired by Waters' essay quoted above, because in 1955 he fashioned his own surfboard and became the first to surf the Bore. Thousands more have followed in 'Mad Jack's wake, and the Bore is now commonly surfed using longboards, kayaks and paddleboards.

In 2006, Steve King managed to board surf for an amazing 12.2km, but most rides are much shorter as the Bore changes shape along its course. Paddlers washing off the front wave are often able to catch and surf the following waves. Short paddlecraft are not much use here, select something with a bit of speed.

The Bore is typically surfed from these spots, in upstream order:

Newnham SO 693 120 / GL14 1BH – Paddle from Newnham car park or the river left bank, taking careful note of the powerful and confused ebb currents, to await the Bore at the sandbar in the centre of the river or a little further downstream. Potentially surfable all the way to Epney.

The Severn Bore Inn SO 754 153 / GL2 8JX – Await the Bore at the first corner downstream

*His nickname is valid: he wielded a broadsword against the Nazis and was the only allied soldier to kill an enemy with a longbow.

of the pub. Paul Robertson: *"Probably the most popular spot, with the least makeable wave. You need to commit to sitting tight to the bank in a crowd of other craft, with branches sticking out from the banks – quite sketchy."*

Over Bridge SO 816 195 / GL2 8BZ - Access the spot from Horseshoe Drive, as noted above. Be quick to exit the wave after passing beneath Maisemore Bridge, as Maisemore Weir lurks upstream. Paul Robertson: *"Often the most consistent wave, regularly breaking river wide."*

All three spots above are accessed by negotiating the muddy foreshore, which needs obvious care. They are all on the river right (north) bank of the Severn; this makes it possible, with car support, experience and a bit of planning to surf all three spots on one single Bore.

Surfing the Bore is a hazardous undertaking. The Bore surges relentlessly over or through overhanging branches, roots, rocks, metalwork and collapsing banks. Along its path it scoops up and carries floating debris including oil drums, pallets, drowned livestock and even whole trees. A more immediate hazard is that you are highly unlikely to be surfing alone. The Bore is usually packed with surfers riding

Cheesy surfs the Bore

Waving at people in their gardens, daring to try paddle tricks; my first bore ride was quite surreal. My friend never caught it, so I surfed a muddy wave, that inexplicably travelled upstream, on my own. For two or three miles, with no idea where it would end, or how I would get back; as a sixteen-year-old, it felt damn cool.

The second time, many years later, was with a magazine editor. After much talk in the pub, we got on the water, and sat waiting ... and waiting ... and waiting. Eventually giving up, we discovered we'd misread the tide tables and hadn't even got the right day – as paddlesports industry professionals it was something we agreed to keep humbly quiet about!

Recently, living at the confluence of Wye and Severn, I surfed the bore regularly; obsessively even. It was like learning an instrument and finding its nuances; getting the ride required know-how of river conditions, movement of sandbars and wind. I migrated to surf kayaks, fins removed so as not to get caught on mud flats; fast enough to plane when the wave fades, but mostly able to rip turns when it is on! I had some great rides, managing about six and a half miles at best. It's very addictive.

With a healthy dollop of surf tourists and novelty river craft lining up alongside dedicated regulars, it's tricky to get a decent ride. I surfed more and more at night, usually on my own. Sabrina, the locals' affectionate name for the river, takes on a different persona in the dark. The whole experience gets a little mystical and senses are heightened by the frisson of danger.

elbow to elbow, meaning that you'll have to be skilled enough to maintain control in an enclosed space, lest you injure or are injured by a fellow rider. No matter how stressful or intimidating this proximity might seem, it is essential that you are able to maintain courtesy and respect for your fellow Bore-riders. The Bore is no place for egos!

Should the Severn Bore experience leave you wanting more bore-dom (see what I did there?), then the next step is to book a flight to visit the Qiantang River at Hangzhou in China, the largest bore on Earth at ten metres high. Perhaps first warm up on the Amazon River's Pororoca in Brazil, a mere four metre high wave.

Further information

www.gloucesterharbourtrustees.org.uk – Gloucester Harbour Trustees publish a downloadable detailed guide to surfing the Bore.
www.thesevernbore.co.uk / www.severn-bore.co.uk – predictions of Bore sizes and arrival times.

A night with Sabrina

With cold creeping into my bones, sitting alone on the water, I wait for Sabrina to wake up and begin another night's dalliance. A stickler for timekeeping, marked by the loud applause of water breaking in the distance, she roars her coming. Amplified by night, she ripples like a snake across the sandbars and crashes mightily through trees and foliage.

Fuelled by the magnetism of the moon, she surges through the channels and onto the mud flats, gathering herself up, becoming tall and forming into the shape of a wave in front of me. Sometimes lit by silvery moon beams showing off her magnificence, at other times she remains coy, cloaked, hidden.

As you begin to dance, she calls a tune. Fast, sweaty, dirty – sometimes she exhausts you, as she twists quickly from side to side, changing shape as she goes. Other times she plays a slow tempo and frustrates, passing you by, barely offering a glimpse of herself as she moves upriver – no second chance.

You never know how long she might let you dance; maybe just metres, maybe for miles. She is always powerful. Often gathering toys and trinkets as she goes, holding on to them until bored ... you included. Fine, dark and brown, she is highly charged; if she likes you, her kisses do not wash away easily.

When she's had enough of you, her back turns, excitedly rushing away like a reveller at a noisy carnival parade; leaving you to take the walk of shame back, scrambling up mudbanks and clambering through hedges as she continues to dance.

Then, like a partygoer with a curfew, the ocean eventually calls her back. She turns, sullenly, this time moving more slowly and thoughtfully, heading back downstream ... until next time.

Paul 'Cheesy' Robertson is a former Freestyle Kayaking World Champion and Surf Kayaking World Championships Silver Medallist.

Llandinam Bridge.

Launching on the Severn

"Half of the joy of canoeing is getting away early in the morning"
W.G. Luscombe and L.J. Bird, *Canoeing*, 1948

The Severn is well-served with points from which to potentially launch your paddlecraft. The list of waypoints and launch points in this chapter is by no means exhaustive, but hopefully offers a wide enough range of possibilities to give access to all sections. Unless a launch point is indicated as being appropriate for larger groups, assume that there is only space, or it is only appropriate, for a handful of paddlers and a small number of vehicles. Exercise discretion, act respectfully and don't linger whilst changing or getting organised at these places; not because you aren't allowed to be there, but because you want to be welcomed back there (some spots are in small communities, for example). Some launch points are little more than narrow gaps in the bank undergrowth, and it is not uncommon to find them in use by anglers; in which case, you should have arrived earlier! Marinas have not been included, being geared towards larger craft and usually involving a launch fee.

It should be noted that not all spots listed are on public land; check details in the section description.

Severn Uplands

Waypoint	Grid reference	Post code	Possible launch point?	Larger groups?	Distance from previous waypoint	Distance from source of Severn
Source of the Severn	SN 822 899		N	N	0km	0km
Rhaeadr Blaen-hafren	SN 836 884		N	N	2.4km	2.4km
Rhyd-y-benwch car park	SN 857 869	SY18 6PT	N	N	3km	5.4km
Severn-Break-its-Neck Waterfall	SN 863 867	SY18 6PT	N	N	1km	6.4km
Layby below Severn-Break-its-Neck Water-fall	SN 868 867	SY18 6PT	Y, RR	N	500m	6.9km
Geufron	SN 881 855	SY18 6PT	Y, RR	N	2.1km	9km
Old Hall Bridge	SN 908 845	SY18 6PW	Y, RR	N	3.3km	12.3km
Llanidloes	SN 954 847	SY18 6HG	Y, RL/ RR	N	4.6km	17.9km
Dolwen Bridge	SN 997 851	SY18 6LX	Y, RR	N	3.5km	23.4km
Llandinam Bridge	SO 025 885	SY17 5DW	Y, RL	N	5km	28.4km
Caersws	SO 032 917	SY17 5DX	Y, RR	N	5.2km	33.6km
Newtown	SO 110 916	SY16 1AA	Y, RR	Y	9.3km	46.9km
Cil Gwrgan Bridge	SO 143 933	SY16 3AQ	Y, RR	N	6km	51.9km
Caerhowel Bridge	SO 196 981	SY15 6RT	Y, RR	N	8.4km	60.3km
Cil-Cewydd Bridge	SJ 227 040	SY21 8RT	Y, RL/ RR	N	10.5km	70.8km
Leighton Bridge	SJ 236 069	SY21 8FJ	Y, RL	N	4km	74.8km
Pool Quay	SJ 247 099	SY21 9JT	Y, RL	Y	5.6km	80.4km
Rhyd-esgyn	SJ 278 148	SY21 9LD	Y, RL	N	10km	90.4km
Llandrinio Bridge	SJ 298 169	SY22 6SG	Y, RL	N	4.6km	95km
Crewgreen Bridge	SJ 329 157	SY5 9BS	Y, RL/ RR	Y	5.2km	100.2km
Montford Bridge (Wingfield Caravan Park)	SJ 432 152	SY4 1EB	Y, RR	Y	16.3km	116.5km
Shrewsbury (Frankwell Footbridge)	SJ490128	SY3 8HQ	Y, RR	Y	18.8km	135.3km

Middle Severn

Waypoint	Grid reference	Post code	Possible launch point?	Larger groups?	Distance from previous waypoint	Distance from source of Severn
Shrewsbury (Shrewsbury Weir)	SJ 500 130	SY1 2JW	Y, RL	Y	3.4km	138.7km
Atcham Bridges	SJ 540 093	SY5 6QH	Y, RR	N	10.9km	149.6km
Cressage Bridge	SJ 594 045	SY5 6BZ	Y, RL	N	12.2km	161.8km
Buildwas	SJ 648 044	TF8 7BN	Y, RL	N	8.4km	170.2km
Ironbridge (Dale End Park)	SJ 665 036	TF8 7DG	Y, RL	Y	2.6km	172.8km
Jackfield (Half Moon Inn)	SJ 690 028	TF8 7LP	Y, RR	Y	2.2km	175km
Coalport (Jackfield & Coalport Memorial Bridge)	SJ 693 026	TF8 7HR	Y, RL	N	400m	175.4km
Jackfield (Boat Inn)	SJ 701 021	TF8 7JA	Y, RR	N	100m	175.5km
Coalport (Coalport Bridge)	SJ 701 021	TF8 7JA	Y, RL	N	900m	176.4km
Bridgnorth (Southwell Riverside)	SO 720 935	WV16 4JZ	Y, RR	N	10.6km	187km
Bridgnorth (Severn Park)	SO 719 933	WV15 5AF	Y, RL	Y	100m	187.1km
Hampton Loade	SO 747 865	WV15 6HD	Y, RL	Y	9km	196.1km
Hampton	SO 746 864	WV16 6NU	Y, RR	N	0km	196.1km
Highley	SO 750 830	WV16 6NU	Y, RR	N	4km	200.1km
Upper Arley	SO 763 802	DY12 1RY	Y, RL	Y	3.7km	203.8km
Bewdley (Gardners Meadow car park)	SO 789 751	DY12 2DU	Y, RR	Y	6.4km	210.2km
Bewdley (Ribbesford Road)	SO 789 740	DY12 2TQ	Y, RR	N	1.6km	211.8km
Stourport (Areley Lane)	SO 806 711	DY13 0AB	Y, RR	N	4km	215.8km
Stourport (Severn Meadows car park)	SO 806 711	DY13 8RB	Y, RL	Y	0km	215.8km
The Burf	SO 813 678	DY13 0RY	Y, RR	N	3km	219.8km

Severn Vale

Waypoint	Grid reference	Post code	Possible launch point?	Larger groups?	Distance from previous waypoint	Distance from source of Severn
Holt Fleet Lock	SO 823 634	WR6 6NW	Y, RL	Y	5.3km	225.1km
The Slip	SO 835 576	WR3 7NF	Y, RL	N	7.2km	232.3km
Worcester (Waterworks Road)	SO 840 564	WR1 3EZ	Y, RL	Y	1.4km	233.7km
Worcester (Grand Stand Road)	SO 844 551	WR1 3EJ	Y, RL	Y	1.7km	235.4km
Worcester Bridge (north)	SO 846 548	WR1 3NY	Y, RL	Y	400m	235.8km
Worcester Bridge (south)	SO 846 547	WR2 4RL	Y, RR	Y	0km	235.8km
Worcester (Severn Street)	SO 848 542	WR1 2NF	Y, RL	N	600m	236.4km
Worcester (Diglis Locks)	SO 847 533	WR5 3BS	Y, RL	Y	1km	237.4km
Kempsey	SO 847 491	WR5 3JH	Y, RL	N	4.5km	241.9km
Pixham Ferry Lane	SO 841 485	WR2 4TQ	Y, RR	N	800m	242.7km
Clevelode	SO 835 468	WR13 6PD	Y, RR	N	2.6km	245.3km
Severn Stoke	SO 848 444	WR8 9JQ	Y, RL	Y	3.2km	248.5km
Hanley Castle	SO 845 419	WR8 0BS	Y, RR	Y	3km	251.5km
Upton-upon-Severn	SO 852 407	WR8 0HG	Y, RR	Y	1.3km	252.8km
Lower Lode Inn	SO 879 317	GL19 4RE	Y, RR	Y	1.8km	264.6km
Tewkesbury (Lower Lode)	SO 880 317	GL20 5GL	Y, RL	Y	0km	264.6km
Deerhurst	SO 867 299	GL19 4BX	Y, RL	N	2.3km	266.9km
Yew Tree Inn	SO 865 297	GL19 4EQ	Y, RR	N	200m	267.1km
Haw Bridge	SO 844 278	GL19 4HJ	Y, RL	Y	3.2km	270.3km
Red Lion	SO 847 258	GL2 9LW	Y, RL	N	1.7km	272km
Ashleworth Quay	SO 818 250	GL19 4HZ	Y, RR	N	3.5km	275.5km
Maisemore Bridge	SO 816 211	GL2 8ES	Y, RR	N	4.5km	280km
Gloucester (Docks)	SO 827 186	GL1 2JN	Y, RL	N	7.9km	283.4km

Waypoint	Grid reference	Post code	Possible launch point?	Larger groups?	Distance from previous waypoint	Distance from source of Severn
Gloucester (Castle Meads car park)	SO 823 182	GL1 2NH	Y, RR	N	200m	283.6km
Strand Lane	SO 715 132	GL14 1PG	Y, RR	N	26km	306km
Newnham	SO 693 120	GL14 1BH	Y, RR	Y	2.5km	308.5km
Sharpness Lifeboat Station	SO 667 029	GL13 9UB	Y, RL	N	18.2km	326.7km
Severn Road Bridge	ST 555 904		N	N	18.9km	345.6km
Second Severn Crossing / end of the River Severn	ST 507 867		N	N	6.4km	352km

Severn Uplands breakfast.

Camping

"When the tent was up and the fires burning we bathed in the weir pool and dined as one dines in camp, and turned in while the dusk was yet falling and the sun had not long set behind the Berwyn Hill."

The Heart of England by Waterway, William Bliss, 1933

Camping beside water is just about the finest thing you can do with your life (apart of course from paddling on water). The Severn has a decent number of campsites along its banks from which to either base yourself or, given that they are helpfully spaced apart, plan a multi-day expedition around. It also has many large caravan and holiday parks, which may or may not be your thing.

There is no legally enshrined right to 'wild camp' in most of England and Wales. If this practice is something that you wish to learn more about, start by looking up the *Wild Camping Code of Conduct* online.

Listed overleaf are campsites, hostels and 'glamping' options along or near the Severn. Most are closed over the winter months. Be mindful that campsite details change more regularly than any other aspect of this guidebook's information; campsites open, campsites close. Included below are a number of caravan parks who have indicated that they accept tents; this may change, sometimes on a whim! Some sites open in some years, but not in others. Some sites listed are little more than farmer's fields; whether they open to you may simply depend upon the politeness of your tone when calling. Also, some of the sites become very busy and are booked up months in advance; you are strongly recommended to call ahead and check what is available before setting off!

Severn Uplands

Name	Number on maps	Section(s)	Grid reference	Post code	Beside river? (River right, river left)
Belan Bluebell Woods	1	1, 2	SN 941 819	SY18 6QL	N, RR
Ty Llewelyn Glamping & Camping	2	1, 2	SN 955 800	SY18 6QD	N, RR
Plasnewydd Bunkhouse	3	1, 2	SN968840	SY18 6LA	N, RR
Dol Llys Farm	4	1, 2	SN 963 857	SY18 6JA	Y, RL
Smithy Park	5	4	SO 159 948	SY15 6ND	Y, RR
Glan Hafren Camping	6	4	SO 168 963	SY15 6NA	Y, RL
Bron Hafren	7	4, 5	SO 198 982	SY15 6RT	Y, RL
Mill Field, Glanhafren	8	5	SJ 228 044	SY21 8RS	Y, RL
Severn Caravan Park	9	5	SJ 230 044	SY21 8RT	Y, RR
The Green Dragon Inn and Campsite	10	5	SJ 250 088	SY21 8SS	N, RR
The Boat House Farm	11	6	SJ 298 169	SY22 6SG	Y, RL
Haimwood Shooting Ground	12	6	SJ 317 162	SY22 6SQ	Y, RL
Big Bear Lodge	13	6	SJ 328 175	SY10 8PH	N, RL
Church House Caravan & Camping	14	6	SJ 332 166	SY10 8PJ	N, RL
Brook House Farm	15	6	SJ 330 156	SY5 9BS	Y, RR
Buckley Farm Campsite	16	6	SJ 362 170	SY4 1BU	Y, RL
Preston Montford Field Studies Centre	17	6	SJ4 32 143	SY4 1DX	Y, RR
Wingfield Caravan Park	18	6, 7	SJ 432 152	SY4 1EB	Y, RR
Bicton House Camping and Caravanning	19	6, 7	SJ 446 146	SY3 8EH	N, RR
Bickley Coppice Scout and Guide Campsite	20	7	SJ 438 159	SY3 8EU	Y, RR
The Isle Estate wild camping area	21	7	SJ 464 166	SY3 8EE	Y, RR
Oxon Hall Touring Park	22	7	SJ 456 137	SY3 5FB	N, RR
Greenhous West Mid Showground	23	7	SJ 484 133	SY1 2PF	Y, RL
Coton Hill Farm	24	7, 8	SJ 490 137	SY1 2PB	N, RL

Phone	Website / email	Notes
01686 412461	www.belanbluebells.com	Camping and glamping options, 2km from the river.
01686 411222	www.tyllewelyn.com	Camping and glamping options, 4km from the river.
01686 412431	www.plasnewyddbunkhouse.co.uk	1.5km from the river. Bunkhouse.
01686 412694	www.dolllyscaravancampsite.co.uk	Just downstream of Llanidloes.
01686 630657	www.smithypark.co.uk	
07826 333632	www.kingfisherkayakhire.com/information	'Back to basics' camping
07500 660004	www.campingandcaravanningclub.co.uk	Camping and caravanning club site. Downstream of Caerhowell Bridge.
01938 553200		Only by prior arrangement. A field with no facilities.
01938 580238	www.severnbunkhouse.co.uk	Bunkhouse available.
01938 553076	www.facebook.com/Greendragonandkitchen/	300m from Buttington Bridge.
07814 598591	www.boathousecamping.com	Beside Llandrinio Bridge.
01691 830764	www.haimwoodshooting.com	Limited facilities. By prior arrangement, lest you get shot.
07711 312103	www.bigbearlodge.co.uk	Glamping pods, 2km from Crewgreen Bridge.
01691 682754	www.churchhousemelverley.co.uk	Beside the River Vyrnwy. Closed temporarily(?) during Covid.
01743 884024	www.brookhousefarm.net	Camping, glamping and B&B options.
01743 741336	davies.153@btinternet.com	
01743 852040	www.field-studies-council.org	Dorm accommodation.
07853 934379	www.thewingfieldcaravanpark.co.uk	Upstream of Montford Bridge.
01743 850054	www.bictoncountryhousepursuits.co.uk	1.5km from Montford Bridge.
	bickleycoppicewarden@hotmail.co.uk	Scouts and guides only.
07976 443742	www.the-isle-estate.co.uk	Only with prior permission from Mr Tate. B&B available.
01743 340868	www.morris-leisure.co.uk	1km from the river.
01743 289831	www.westmidshowground.com	Within Shrewsbury. Glamping options available.
07810 356797	www.campingandcaravanningclub.co.uk	Tiny, in Shrewsbury, 250m from the river.

Middle Severn

Name	Number on maps	Section(s)	Grid reference	Post code	Beside river? (River right, river left)
Love2Stay	25	8	SJ 522 106	SY5 6QS	Y, RR
Paradise Meadow	26	8	SJ 537 095	SY5 6QG	Y, RL
Ismore Coppice Wild Campground	27	8	SJ 558 090	SY5 6QZ	Y, RL
Buildwas Park Farm	28	8	SJ 632 041	TF8 7BP	Y, RR
Pool View Caravan Park	29	8, 9	SJ 651 035	TF8 7BS	N, RR
Irongorge Camping	30	8, 9	SJ 662 045	TF8 7EY	N, RL
YHA Ironbridge Coalbrookdale	31	8, 9	SJ 670 041	TF8 7NR	N, RL
YHA Ironbridge Coalport	32	9	SJ 695 024	TF8 7HT	Y, RL
Bridgnorth Rugby Club	33	9, 10	SO 719 933	WV15 5AF	Y, RL
Halfway House Inn	34	10	SO708908	WV16 5LS	N, RR
The Unicorn Inn & Campsite	35	10	SO 746 867	WV16 6BN	Y, RR
High Class Camping	36	10	SO 757 793	DY12 3LX	N, RR
Stars and Wild	37	10	SO 782 764	DY12 1AW	N, RL
Hopley's Family Camping	38	10, 11	SO 769 747	DY12 2QL	N, RR
Haye Farm Sleeping Barn	39	10, 11	SO 779 740	DY12 2TP	N, RR
Lickhill Manor Caravan Park	40	11	SO 795 718	DY13 8RL	Y, RL
Amber's Bell Tents	41	11	SO 831 695	DY13 9SA	N, RL
Brant Farm Caravan Park	42	11	SO799658	WR6 6TD	N, RR
Riverholme Sky Tent	43	11	SO 813 636	WR6 6TA	Y, RR
Holt Fleet Farm Camping and Caravanning	44	11, 12	SO 823 634	WR6 6NW	Y, RL

Phone	Website / email	Notes
01743 282400	www.love2stay.co.uk	Glamping resort.
01743 239239	charlief-b@balfours.co.uk	No facilities, only by prior arrangement with Longnor Estate. Upstream of Atcham Bridges.
	attingham.camping@nationaltrust.org.uk	Run by the National Trust, on the Attingham Park estate.
07970 903719		No facilities, only by prior arrangement with Mrs Helen Jones.
01952 433182	www.poolviewcaravanpark.com	900m from the river.
07811 340830	www.irongorgecamping.co.uk	350m from the river. Camping and glamping options.
0345 371 9325	www.yha.org.uk	650m from the river. Youth Hostel.
0345 371 9325	www.yha.org.uk	Youth Hostel.
07970 019306	www.bridgnorthrfc.co.uk	Limited facilities, only by prior arrangement.
01746 762670	www.halfwayhouseinn.co.uk	
01746 861515	www.unicornhamptonloade.co.uk	At Hampton Loade.
01299 271507	www.highclasscamping.co.uk	1.5km from the river. Glamping site.
07543 768363	www.starsandwild.co.uk	'Glampsite', 150m from the river.
01299 402173	www.hopleyscamping.co.uk	2km from the river. Camping and glamping options.
07732489195	www.haye-farm.co.uk	1.5km from the river. Bunkhouse.
01299 871041	www.hillandale.co.uk/our-parks/lickhill-manor-caravan-park	At Stourport-on-Severn.
07818 421982	www.ambersbelltents.co.uk	1km from the river. Glamping tents.
01905 621008	www.brantfarmcaravan.co.uk	1.5km from the river.
07544725326	www.riverholmeskytent.com	Treetop glamping (yes, that is a thing).
01905 620512	www.holt-fleet-farm.edan.io	Beside Holt Fleet Lock.

Severn Vale

Name	Number on maps	Section(s)	Grid reference	Post code	Beside river? (River right, river left)
The Wharf Caravan Park and Fisheries	45	11, 12	SO 826 634	WR6 6NN	Y, RL
Mill House Caravan Site & Boatyard	46	12	SO 846 600	WR3 7SE	N, RL
Worcester Glamping	47	12	SO840527	WR2 4BS	N, RR
Riverside Caravan Park	48	12	SO 835 460	WR13 6PE	Y, RR
Turk's End Farm	49	13	SO 863 422	WR8 9DA	N, RL
Fish Meadow Camping	50	13	SO 851 408	WR8 0PB	Y, RL
Dawley's Caravan Site	51	13	SO 882 351	GL20 6EQ	N, RL
The Willows	52	13, 14	SO 878 317	GL19 4RE	Y, RR
Lower Lode Inn	53	13, 14	SO 879 317	GL19 4RE	Y, RR
Haw Bridge Inn	54	14	SO 844 278	GL19 4HJ	Y, RR
Red Lion Inn Camping & Caravan Park	55	14	SO 848 258	GL2 9LW	Y, RL
The Glamping Orchard	56	15	SO 760 138	GL2 3SW	N, RL
Apple Orchard	57	15	SO 727 149	GL14 1PH	N, RR
Gramp's Field	58	15	SO 743 138	GL14 1QS	Y, RR
Passage Farm	59	15	SO 698 112	GL2 7JR	Y, RL
The Anchorage	60	15	SO 689 099	GL14 1ED	Y, RR
West End Farm and Campsite	61	15	SO 705 102	GL2 7JL	Y, RL
Severn Valley Touring Caravan and Camping Site	62	15	SO 702 084	GL14 1EJ	N, RR
Elm Farm	63	15	SO 751 042	GL2 7AN	N, RL
Tudor Caravan Park	64	15	SO 727 042	GL2 7BP	N, RL
Forest Oak Farm	65	15	SO 657 052	GL15 4LN	N, RR

Phone	Website / email	Notes
	www.thewharfcaravanparkandfisheries.co.uk	Downstream of Holt Fleet Bridge.
01905 451283	www.millhousecaravanandcamping.co.uk	Beside the River Salwarpe and Droitwich Barge Canal.
07539690155	www.worcesterglamping.co.uk	Yurt glamping, close to the River Teme and 1km from the Severn.
01684 310475	www.riverside-park.co.uk	
07795 32478	www.turksendfarm.co.uk	1.3km from the river.
07788 441612	www.fishmeadowcamping.co.uk	At Upton-upon-Severn, often used for festival events.
01684 292622	www.facebook.com/DawleysCaravanPark	400m from the river.
07707 031828	chris@newandusedboat.co.uk	Behind Lower Lode Inn.
01684 293224	www.lowerlodeinn.co.uk	Beside Lower Lode Inn.
07811 535239	www.campingandcaravanningclub.co.uk	Adults only, doesn't always accept tents.
01452 731810		
07974 174534	www.glampingorchard.co.uk	Glamping only, 500m from the river.
01452 760618	www.appleorchardcampsite.co.uk	2.5km from the river. Glamping pods available.
07778 901007		700m from the river.
07505 807540	www.passagefarm.co.uk	
01594 369775	www.theanchorage.site	Camping and glamping options.
01452 740419		
01594 516537	www.severnvalleytouring.co.uk	1km from the water. Camping and glamping options.
01453 825332	www.campingandcaravanningclub.co.uk	3km from the river, near Slimbridge.
01453 890483	www.tudorcaravanpark.com	1.5km from the water, beside the Gloucester and Sharpness Canal.
01594 840322	www.forestoakfarm.co.uk	3km from the river.

Brynderwen Bridge.

Culture and Landscape: The Story of the River Severn

"The traveller by water in England cannot escape an awareness of the past since he himself is moving at a slower and more reflective tempo than those on the shore."

E. W. Hunter-Christie, in *Portraits of Rivers*, 1953

Geology

The oldest rocks on the Severn are, perhaps aptly, found at its source in the Cambrian Mountains of Mid-Wales. It flows over Ordovician and Silurian* mudstone, grits, slates and shales comprised of deep ocean sediments from the Early Palaeozoic era (485-420 mya). Severn-Break-its-Neck Waterfall descends across the boundary of resistant sandstone into an eroded plunge pool of softer muds, silts and sands. The Severn's north-east course approximately follows the strata of this underlying hard rock. Near Welshpool, hard, igneous (volcanic) rocks intrude; a 260m-thick layer of dolerite tops the Breidden Hills, visible from the river at Criggion Quarry. The small grain size of the dolerite indicates that the magma cooled relatively quickly.

As the Severn meanders across the North Shropshire Plain, the bedrock is replaced by softer, riverine sandstones from the Permian period (299 to 251 mya), visible in the reddish scoured banks approaching Shrewsbury. The sandstone is submerged beneath a thick layer of glacial deposits; gravel and silty alluvium soils laid down in the Quaternary period (2.5 mya to the present). This has made for some interesting challenges in Shrewsbury's engineering, where the Darwin Centre stands on 30m piles and the High Street is built around a glacial 'kettle hole' formed when a stranded block of ice was surrounded by glacial outwash.

The Middle Severn once again passes through Ordovician and Silurian rocks before meeting bands of younger Carboniferous (359 to 299 mya) strata, at Shrewsbury and between Ironbridge and Bewdley, where the river has deeply incised the hills of Wenlock Edge. The deposits of tropical Carboniferous coal, iron ore and limestone exposed at Ironbridge Gorge changed history!

*Named after the Ordovices and Silures, pre-Roman Celtic tribes who inhabited the Severn valley.

Garden Cliff.

Below Ironbridge Gorge and through the Severn Vale, the Severn flows over and through sedimentary rocks which span eons of geological eras, tending to become 'younger' in age as you progress downriver; Carboniferous (359–299 mya), Permian (299–251 mya) and Triassic (252–201 mya). This stratum is most recognisable in the sandstone outcrops which intermittently loom above shallow reefs in the river; High Rock at Bridgnorth is Triassic flash flood, pebble beds on top of Permian desert sandstone, the windblown sands of the cliffs at Quatford are Permian and riverine Redstone Rock at Stourport is Triassic.

The even more youthful geology of the Jurassic (201-145 mya) underlies the Severn Vale from Tewkesbury onwards, with outcrops of the famous, fossil-rich Blue Lias. This consists of layered limestone, mudstone and siltstone marine sediments exposed at cliff sites along the estuary such as Garden Cliff and Hock Cliffs, also forming reefs on the riverbed. The bedrock is covered with Quaternary alluvium, sand and gravel, and the river is lined by fluvioglacial terraces consisting of glacial meltwater deposits including boulders weighing more than a tonne. This relates to the huge increase in the volume of the Severn when glaciers rerouted the river southwards. The subsequent erosion and deposition, between 25,000 to 10,000 years ago, created giant fans of material spreading south from the Cotswolds onto the Severn plain.

The course of the River Severn

The Severn in its present form is remarkably young; possibly less than 10,000 years old. The river was previously much shorter, following its current course as far as Cressage before trending north to reach the present-day location of the Irish Sea between Wirral and North Wales; the lower valley of the River Dee was formerly occupied by the Severn.

During the Devensian glacial period (from 25,000 up to 18,000 years ago), glaciers moved south and blocked the Severn's northerly course. Around 42% of the present river was submerged by ice, sufficient for the transportation of the volcanic Bellstone, a glacial erratic displayed beside the Morris Hall in central Shrewsbury, from either Snowdonia or the Lake District. It's postulated that an ice-dammed lake formed north of Wenlock Edge,

The purported site of Lake Lapworth, from Breidden Hill.

dubbed 'Lake Lapworth'. Eventually (possibly as recently as 10,000 years ago) the lake overtopped and cut through Wenlock Edge, forming Ironbridge Gorge and draining south into an existing, unglaciated river valley at Apley.

An alternative scenario proposed more recently by geologists is that Lake Lapworth may never have existed, at least not on the scale previously imagined. Instead, Ironbridge Gorge was formed by a sub-glacial river escaping from beneath an icesheet. The Severn Trench has been discovered up to 120m below the current surface level, scoured from rock under immense pressure: even flowing uphill at points!

The modern river is of course not static; the bed of the Severn Estuary has risen by 1.7m since Roman times, the Western Channel at Gloucester was possibly only formed in the fifteenth century and a number of the Severn Uplands meanders have only been formed, or cut off, during the last century.

History

The Severn's human history has been defined, from prehistory onwards, by geography. It forms both a physical boundary between England and Wales, and a routeway for industry and trade extending from the Atlantic into the Midlands and Mid-Wales. The settlements along its banks developed both to control its crossing points and to prosper from its trade.

Prehistory

Hundreds of pairs of footprints have been discovered along the muddy shore past the Second Severn Crossing bridge at Magor Pill,

Redwick and Goldcliff in South Wales. The footprints, which can be individually identified as being made by men, women and children, were pressed into soft clay around 6,500 years ago. These Mesolithic families, whose fishing and foraging activities were inadvertently preserved in deep time, offer our earliest connection with the Severn's human history. Pollen records have revealed that the flood plains of the Severn valley were already being cleared of their alder and willow by 6,800BC, with some crops sown. The Neolithic period, when farming replaced the hunter-gatherer lifestyle, commenced along the Severn after 3,500BC. The now-settled populace constructed monuments such as standing stones and henges (circular earthen banks). The Severn Uplands in Wales are especially rich in these monuments, or at least they have been better preserved there. Carreg Wen (white stone) is a lone standing stone overlooking the Severn's headwaters on Plynlimon. There are traces of barrows and a henge beside the river at Dyffryn near Garthmyl, and crop marks revealed a similar, riverside ritual landscape consisting of a henge and cursus (long earthen bank) outside Welshpool, since disturbed by bypass works.

The Bronze Age, starting around 2,500BC, is usually characterised by goods being ritually deposited in rivers and marshes. However, few such deposits have been found in the Severn, which seemingly had a different culture to that of east-flowing rivers such as the Thames. The river was certainly well-populated and

The Wrekin from Cressage Bridge.

was already a focus of trade and transport, as indicated by the remains of a plank boat discovered beside the estuary at Caldicot.

The Iron Age (starting around 800BC) is represented along the Severn Uplands by numerous, earthen hillforts atop hills overlooking the river, such as those at Cefn Carnedd near Llandinam and Breidden Hill. The Wrekin's spectacularly located hillfort was probably the capital of the Cornovii tribe who dominated the region.

The Romans

The Romans fully grasped the Severn's geographical significance. According to chronicler Tacitus, reaching the Severn frontier was an objective of their 43AD conquest, following which, they used it as a conduit to invade Wales. They burned the Wrekin hillfort in 47AD and around 50AD, Caractacus made his last stand against their invasion, possibly at Caersws (see page 65). The Roman victors established frontier forts along the river, traces of which are visible at Caersws and Forden Gaer. Viroconium (Wroxeter) eventually became a major city (see page 107), additionally

Wroxeter Roman City.

Worcester and Glevum (Gloucester) were founded at crossing points. Traces of a wooden quayside have been discovered at Gloucester. Nearby, Roman road, Ermine Street crossed at the present-day site of Over Bridge. The Romans also seem to have established crossings on the estuary, possibly at Newnham and Aust, site of the Severn Road Bridge. The Aust Goddess is a small bronze statuette found in the cliffs at Aust, thought by some to represent the Roman goddess, Minerva.

The Middle Ages
Saxons and Vikings

The Saxon incursions, following the Roman withdrawal c410AD, didn't extend as far west as the Severn for at least two centuries; in the interim, Viroconium seems to have been occupied by local warlords who built wooden great halls over the Roman ruins.

The Saxon settlements of England eventually spread to the River Severn; a seventh-century conference of bishops declared that the Severn marked the division between the Saxon English and the Celtic British / Welsh. The Saxon Kingdom of Mercia developed to the east of the river, whilst various Welsh Kingdoms, notably Powys, formed to the west and across the Severn Uplands. In reality, the Welsh border was far more fluid and when King Offa of Mercia (757-796) built his famous Dyke *"from the sea right to the sea"* (Bishop Asser), it only briefly followed the Severn, near Buttington (see Section 6).

In the late ninth century the Severn provided an ideal routeway for Viking raiders to penetrate and raid Mercia. 'Danes' sailed up the river repeatedly, establishing camps at Gloucester in 877, Buttington in 893 and Quatford in 895. Æthelflæd, Lady of the Mercians (c870-918), responded by founding *burhs* (fortified towns) at the Severn's key crossing points; Shrewsbury, Bridgnorth, Worcester and Gloucester.

Marcher lords

The Norman Conquest of 1066 was hugely consequential for the culture and landscape of the Severn. William I ('The Conqueror') created Marcher Lordships (from Old English *mearc*: boundary); these were ambitious, Norman nobles installed along the Welsh / English border region (the 'Marches'), given huge power and autonomy to subjugate and invade Wales at their leisure. Roger de Montgomery was installed as Earl of Shrewsbury to control the central Marches. Beginning with the construction of Shrewsbury Castle in 1067, he rapidly built a chain of motte-and-bailey castles along the Severn; extending upstream from Shrewsbury as far as Llandinam and Llanidloes, and downstream to Bridgnorth. The Severn was simply the starting point for Roger de Montgomery, who used it as a base to invade Wales as far south-west as Pembrokeshire! Norman castles were also constructed outside the Marches at crossing points such as Worcester and Gloucester. The Severn's first recorded bridges appeared at such crossing points.

The Marcher lordships existed until abolished by Henry VIII in 1535.

The last Prince of Wales

The Severn Uplands were central to Edward I's subjugation of Wales. In 1267, Henry III met Llywelyn ap Gruffudd ('our last leader') at Rhydwhyman ford (see Section 5) and recognised him as Prince of Wales in the Treaty of Montgomery. However, conflict continued between Llywelyn and the Marcher lords (as evidenced by Dolforwyn Castle, page 72) and in 1277 the new king, Edward I, commenced a series of invasions based from Shrewsbury. The tragic culmination of these wars was the savage execution of Llywelyn's son Dafydd ap Gruffudd at Shrewsbury in 1283. Welsh independence was extinguished, and Wales annexed as a Principality of the English crown. The last Welsh rebellion, that of Owain Glyndwr, had echoes along the Severn; when Henry Percy was defeated by Henry IV at the Battle of Shrewsbury in 1403 (*"on the gentle Severn's sedgy bank"* Shakespeare, *Henry IV Part I*), he was allied with Glyndwr and hoping for reinforcement from him.

Dolforwyn Castle.

Trade and Transport in the Middle Ages

In 1065, Edward the Confessor decreed that the Severn (and Thames, Trent, Ouse) be made navigable, by the destruction of fish weirs. The 'King's high stream of Severn', saw centuries of tension between river traffic and weir owners (usually monasteries); ten different Acts of Parliament between 1346 and 1495 ordered obstructions on the Severn to be, *"utterly pulled down"*. In 1430, the people of Tewkesbury complained about pirates from the Forest of Dean boarding and looting vessels, *"in manner of war, as enemies of a strange country"*. In that same year, Henry VI declared the Severn to be a Navigation, with no tolls or weirs hindering passage.

Buildwas Abbey.

The monasteries

Religious communities were established along the Severn's length during the Middle Ages. They ranged from tiny churches as far upstream as Llanidloes and Llandinam (*llan* denotes an early Christian church) to Llanthony Secunda in Gloucester, which was England's wealthiest Augustinian house. Sites along the river where traces remain include Strata Marcella, Buildwas, Haughmond, Shrewsbury, Bridgnorth, Worcester, Tewkesbury, Gloucester and Llanthony Secunda. Ostensibly built to practise and preach God's word, the monasteries were important economic centres, regulating farming (they had enormous land holdings) and engaging in industry and trade. For example, Strata Marcella near Pool Quay had a weir and watermill,

Gloucester Cathedral.

Buildwas forged iron and traded in wool and Ribbesford Priory at Bewdley required tenants to, *"make hedges for catching fish"*. The monasteries played a leading role in the deforestation of the Middle Severn valley for shipbuilding and charcoal; the forests of Wyre and Dean survive, but placenames such as Cressage (*Christ's oak*) give clues to the Severn woodlands' former extent.

The massive cathedrals at Worcester, Tewkesbury and Gloucester, all remnants of former monasteries, give a sense of their wealth and power. Similarly, note the vast tithe barn at Ashleworth (Section 14).

Fish weirs

Fish weirs were engineered and used on an industrial scale in the Middle Ages, continuing in use through to modern times. Fish weirs (Old English *wera*, fixed structure to catch fish) were built and owned by the monasteries. Lines of v-shaped wattle baskets or nets (*kidells*) were fixed in place by oak piles, with walkways on top. The centre of the river was often left clear, but numerous artificial islands were constructed (*bylets*) with the side channel providing a 'barge gutter' for boats to scrape past. Fish weirs were most commonly built upstream of Ironbridge Gorge. There are 28 artificial bylets in Shropshire alone (Montford, Fitz, Underdale in Shrewsbury, Pimley Manor, Atcham, Wroxeter, Eytonrock, Coundlane ...) and at least 54 fish weirs on the whole, non-tidal Severn! Preston Boats Weir, mentioned in the 1085 *Domesday Book*, remained in use into the 1920s and its outline can still be clearly seen (see Section 8).

On the Severn estuary, huge, cone-shaped baskets called *putts* were laid across the mud and sands in long lines. Above Sharpness, at least ten of these tidal fish traps were still in use into modern times, and there are remains of further early medieval sites; eroded wooden 'stalagmites' can be seen protruding at low water.

The Severn's main catches were salmon and elvers (young eels), the latter netted on the estuary and regarded as an aphrodisiac. Lampreys were also caught; bizarrely, this barely digestible parasite was regarded as

Fish weir at Preston Boats.

a 'royal' dish. Henry III owned weirs near Newnham to catch them, despite the fact that Henry I died of, *"a surfeit of lampreys"*. Gloucester sent lamprey pies to the monarch at Christmas into the nineteenth century, and supplied Queen Elizabeth II with pies until her 2012 Diamond Jubilee.

The Early Modern era

Henry VIII certainly left his mark on the Severn landscape, with the Dissolution of the Monasteries in 1536–41. The monasteries were dismantled and their assets literally stripped away, leaving hulking ruins such as those of Buildwas Priory. The cathedrals managed to survive through 'buy-outs' by locals.

The Civil Wars

The first significant skirmish of the English Civil War took place in Worcester at Powick Bridge in 1642. The final battle between Royalists and Parliamentarians also took place at Worcester, in 1651 (see page 148). Hugh Peters preached that, *"You have been in Worcester, where England's sorrows began,*

◉ *Attingham Hall.*

where they were happily ended.". Through the Civil Wars, the Severn from Worcester upstream was Royalist, whilst the Severn Vale was held by Parliament. Upton-upon-Severn, caught in between, reputedly saw more skirmishes than any other spot. Many bridges were damaged along the Severn, with drawbridges added.

Many castles, such as Shrawardine, were demolished or slighted following the Civil Wars. Others, like Powis, were converted to stately homes. The nobility (and also those newly rich from industry and trade) now preferred to live in absurdly vast mansions surrounded by landscaped parks. Over the following two centuries, these proliferated along the banks of the Severn, with examples at Loton, Attingham, Cound, Apley, Dudmaston and Severn House (which replaced Hanley Castle). Sir Thomas Habington smugly described the new mansions as, *"the precious diamonds in the coronet of our County, giving light to the inferiors how to direct their lives"* (*A Survey of Worcestershire*, 1640s).

The Industrial Age

Ironbridge is known as, 'the cradle of the Industrial Revolution' on account of the remarkable achievements of the Darby iron-making dynasty during the eighteenth century (see page 119). Ironbridge's iron works, coal mines and tile works were central to a network of industry and trade, in which the Severn was an artery connecting Wales, the Midlands, Bristol and the Atlantic. That said, the Severn was never ideal for commercial use, with a strong current, shoals and reefs along its length, and the Severn Bore bringing silt upriver and making the estuary treacherous. The Industrial Age, spanning up to the present, has (perhaps thankfully) seen only limited success in taming the Severn.

Bridging the Severn

The Industrial Revolution saw an explosion of bridge-building along the Severn. The Iron Bridge was completed in 1779 and was justly described as *"One of the wonders of the world"* (Viscount Torrington, *Diaries*, 1787). In the years

◉ *The Iron Bridge by William Williams 1780.*

Photo | Wikimedia Commons.

209

Victoria Bridge.

1770–1830, eight new crossings were built and all bridges above Stourport were rebuilt. Thomas Penson was prolific along the Severn Uplands in Montgomeryshire, whilst John Fowler, John Gwynne and Thomas Telford left their engineering mark downstream. Telford, as Shropshire County Surveyor, built bridges at Montford, Buildwas, Bridgnorth, Bewdley, Holt Fleet, Tewkesbury and Gloucester.

Trows

At the start of the eighteenth century, the Severn was Europe's busiest river other than the Meuse.

"The river is of great importance on account of its trade, being navigated by vessels of large burden more than 160 miles from the sea, without the assistance of any lock; and from thence into the adjacent countries: also great quantities of grain, pig and bar iron, iron manufactures and earthenwares; as well as wool, hops, cyder and provisions, are constantly exported to Bristol and other places ... ".

George Perry, *A Description of the Severn Valley*, 1758

Perry calculated that 376 trows worked the river in 1758. These were flat-bottomed boats capable of carrying 40-80 tonnes, with sails on masts which could be lowered for bridges. Their shallow-draught design, ideal for the Severn's shoals and its tidal shores, changed little over centuries; around 2,000 were built on the Severn before the advent of the railways. 'Downstream Trows' worked the tidal river from Worcester; the only surviving example is *Spry*, displayed in Ironbridge at Blists Hill Victorian Town. 'Upstream Trows' (also called 'Upriver Trows') were smaller and could reach as far upstream as Pool Quay in winter.

For upstream journeys, trows were hauled by teams of up to twenty 'bow hauliers', harnessed to ropes connected to the top of the mast. They made gruelling progress along the bank, which had no towpath, with one hand gripping the ground. Bow hauliers were infamous for their rough manners and resisted attempts to introduce horses; in 1832 the Riot Act was read at Bewdley and soldiers sent to control them. Telford criticised *"this barbarous and expensive slave-like office"*.

Improving the Severn
Towpath Trusts

Increasing competition from canals, starting with the opening of James Brindley's Staffordshire and Worcestershire Canal in 1772, lead to calls to engineer and tame the Severn, to make it reliably navigable for larger boats and heavier cargos. Archdeacon Plymley noted in 1803, *"the navigation is very much impeded by*

lowness in summer and by floods in winter".
The first step was the establishment of Towpath Trusts between 1772 and 1809; these were companies which built horse towpaths. The replacement of bow hauliers was justified on moral grounds, as their trade was, *"injurious to their manners"* as well as their health. A towpath connected Bewdley and Coalbrookdale (Ironbridge) from 1800, being extended from Gloucester and Shrewsbury by 1812. The Severn Uplands never had a towpath and bow hauling continued unchallenged above Shrewsbury. Despite the towpath, river traffic was always limited. Upstream from Ironbridge, it peaked in the 1820s at roughly one vessel a week. Trows only made the journey downstream intermittently, setting sail in groups (numbering up to 80) when the river became high enough and also fortnightly to meet spring tides at Gloucester.

The Severn Navigation

In 1784, George III's visit to Worcester was marred by trowmen demonstrating against proposals to build sixteen locks between Worcester and Coalbrookdale. Following their lobbying, a Navigation bill was rejected by Parliament in 1786. However, improvements to the tidal river got the go-ahead; a 1793 Act of Parliament lead to the building of the Gloucester and Sharpness Canal, bypassing the worst of the estuary (see page 179).

It was not until 1842 that an Act was finally passed to engineer the Severn Navigation. Between 1843 and 1858, the Severn Commission dredged and canalised the river between Stourport and Gloucester, constructing five locks and weirs. This project was on the wrong side of history and too little, too late: canals, and now railways, were already haemorrhaging traffic from the Severn and in any case, most of the river remained untamed. For example, when the Navigation was completed the rail line to Shrewsbury, now known as the Severn Valley Railway, was already under construction. It no longer made economic sense to transport goods by river;

📷 *Upper Lode Lock.*

"There are often three, four or five months in the year when barges cannot navigate the river with a freight equal to defray the expenses of working them."

John Randall, *Shrewsbury Chronicle*, 1859

River traffic on the new Navigation was never significant in scale. Above Stourport, it steadily declined; trows made their last visits to Pool Quay in the 1850s, 1867 saw just a single trip to Shrewsbury and in 1885, Shropshire's last commercial boat ignominiously sank after hitting Bridgnorth Bridge.

John Randall reflected on how, *"The river is still in a state of nature ... Fords that served our* painted ancestors to make incursions beyond their boundaries, bends almost amounting to circles around which they paddled their canoes, impede navigation still" (*History of Madeley*, 1880).

River traffic continued on the Severn Navigation through the twentieth century. As late as the 1980s, barges and tankers brought oil, coal and timber (from Archangel in Arctic Russia!) to Worcester and Stourport. Today, barges transport aggregates for several kilometres above Tewkesbury, the river's last remaining commercial activity.

Leisure and tourism

The Severn has been on the cultural map since 1715, when the Three Choirs Festival originated, an annual series of concerts rotated between Worcester, Gloucester and Hereford (on the River Wye). Worcester local, Edward Elgar first played violin in the festival. It's not for everyone; in 1788, Madame d'Arblay described it as, *"very long and tedious ... an occasional scream or groan indicated distress or fainting. Some were carried out ..."*.

The advent of railways and decline of river trade from the 1840s opened up the Severn for leisure and tourism. Daytrippers arrived by rail from the Midlands and Black Country. River steamers ferried holidaymakers to resorts such as Holt Fleet. From 1865 and well into the twentieth century, those wishing to make camping trips could hire houseboats, canoes or skiffs from James Baldwin & Co. at Stourport.

Pengwern Boat Club was established in 1835 at Shrewsbury, and other rowing clubs followed. The Welsh Severn saw some interest by adventurous travellers after the railways made the valley accessible, and George Borrow published *Wild Wales* in 1865.

The use of the river for paddlesport was already well-established by the 1930s, when guidebooks were published by both the British Canoe Union and William Bliss (see page 226). Geoffrey Boumphrey described a kayaking expedition in *Down River*, published 1936: a recommended read!

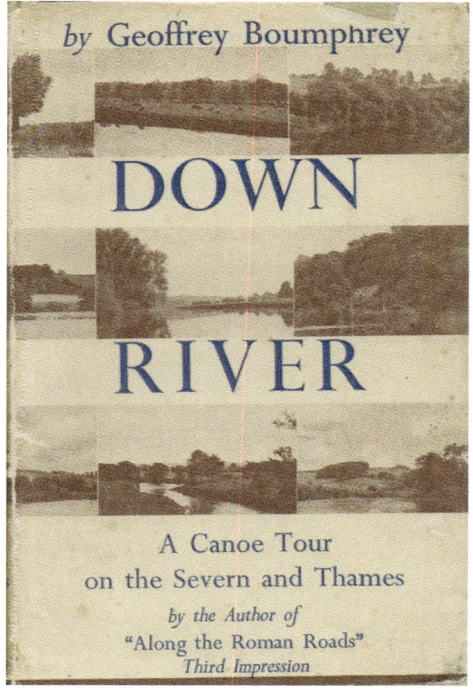
Down River.

Severn Floods

Outlined here are just a handful of the devastating floods wrought by England and Wales' most voluminous river.

The flood of 1483 possibly created the West Channel at Gloucester and also influenced history; it stalled a rebellion against Richard III by the Duke of Buckingham, who could not cross the Severn for ten days. A witness described how, *"Several persons were drowned in their beds, children in cradles swam about in fields, and beasts were drowned, even on the hills"*.

The flood of 1607 was different; an eyewitness described, *"Huge and mighty hills of water"* moving *upstream*. Around two thousand were drowned by the flood, which was likely either a storm surge or a tsunami triggered by an offshore earthquake;

"... in less than five hours space most part of those counties (and especially the places which lay low) were all overflown, and many hundreds of people both men women, and children were then quite devoured, by these outrageous waters, such was the fury of the waves, of the Seas, the one of them driving the other forwards with such force and swiftness, that it is almost incredible for any to believe the same ..."

The flood of 1795 was notable as it brought ice floes downstream. These destroyed or damaged most bridges, with sixteen demolished in Shropshire alone (the Iron Bridge survived). Telford, who subsequently replaced many of the bridges, described how *"The storm of Frost and Snow kept accumulating for two months, after which a very hasty thaw caused a greater inundation than has ever been known in England."*. Another sudden thaw, in 1947, saw the highest *recorded* levels along the Severn, costing £12 million in damage, although it is believed that numerous floods of previous centuries were higher.

The most recent major flood (disclaimer: at time of writing!) was the Great Gloucestershire Flood of June 2007. It was caused by sudden extreme rainfall; 58mm fell in two hours at Bewdley. The subsequent rising waters flooded Tewkesbury Abbey for the first time since 1770. Both the huge waterworks at Mythe and Castle Meads substation were inundated; electricity to the Severn Vale's inhabitants was only saved by the armed forces surrounding Walham sub-station with makeshift barriers. A flow of 1,400 cumecs was extrapolated at Haw Bridge, believed to exceed the 1947 flood. Farcically, Upton and Worcester's flood defence barriers were not raised because they were stored at Kidderminster, and the roads were impassable.

Paddleboarder on Llyn Clywedog.

Wildlife and Environment

"All the way down we had seen heron and swarms of moor-hen and dab-chick and a water-ouzel or two; and more than one kingfisher and reed-warblers had sung their sweet little song, and there had been irises and ragged-robin and water forget-me-not in columns and in carpets."

William Bliss, *The Heart of England by Waterway*, 1933

Nature is in the ascendency along the Severn, as Bliss discovered whilst paddling above Welshpool. The river is effectively a continuous but diverse succession of wildlife habitats, ranging from the untamed meanders of the Severn Uplands, through the regreened industrial sites of the Middle Severn, to the flood-meadows and estuarine flats of the Severn Vale. In recognition of the huge ecological importance of this enclosed wild corridor, there are proposals to designate it as a 'Wildbelt'. The Severn is additionally important because it is relatively untamed. Above Stourport, it flows freely with the features of a natural, almost upland river; the gravel beds, rock reefs and small rapids are precious habitats to a wide range of flora and fauna.

Environmental issues

Reading up on riparian ecology (or indeed any natural history) can be a gloomy experience, as the story is often one of damage and decline. Like any modern natural environment, the Severn does face some significant challenges; however, the picture is not all bleak.

The headwaters

The creation of Hafren Forest, planted across the Severn's headwaters after the First World War, caused problems. The coniferous trees increased the acidity of the river. Furthermore, rainwater ran off quickly along the culverts between the neatly-lined trees, leading to gravel beds being silted over or washed away. The result was reduced salmon populations, and the river remains fishless in the forest. Modern planting is more sympathetic, with buffer zones of deciduous trees planted along the river banks to reduce acidity and create wet woodlands.

The creation of Lake Vyrnwy (1888) and Llyn Clywedog (1967) on the Severn's tributaries regulated the flow, reducing spring and summer 'freshets' which helped salmon and trout migrate upstream. In more recent times, releases are regulated to maintain a sustainable minimum flow.

Pollution

"Through Coalbrookdale, Ironbridge and Coalport the scenery is very definitely industrial ... The river lost its cleanness and hurried over its shallow bed as if to slip from under the film of dirt that dulled its surface. The banks were fouled with lumps of slag and other refuse."

Geoffrey Boumphrey, *Down River*, 1936

Far into the twentieth century, the River Severn suffered heavily from industrial pollution. In addition to the pollution from Ironbridge Gorge, mentioned above by Boumphrey, tributaries like the Stour and Avon discharged effluent from the industrial West Midlands. Pollution reduces the oxygen saturation in a river and causes eutrophication, the process whereby a high level of nutrients develops in a river. Algal blooms cover the surface and shut out light; the more eutrophicated a river, the less species diversity.

Agricultural pollution added to the problem, notably the introduction of the organochloride dieldrin (as a seed dressing and sheep dip) from 1956. This poison, which killed off a range of large fauna including most of the otters, was banned in 1966 but remained in use illegally for decades.

Over the past half century, the river has enjoyed huge improvements in water quality as industry declined and European legislation mandated regulation of water quality. The 'chemical' health of the river is currently rated as 'good' and the ecological health (habitat and species diversity) is rated as 'moderate'.

Attitudes have also changed. Chris Sladden (a

River clean-up below Atcham.

good friend of the author's) explored the Severn Uplands for his 1998 guidebook *The Welsh Rivers* and lamented, *"copious quantities of rubbish in the river"*. That picture of the river as a refuse disposal point is not recognisable today, beyond the occasional traffic cone or football found below large towns.

Development

The engineering of the Severn Navigation from 1843 to 1858 meant that the 68km from Stourport to Gloucester were artificially deepened, with high steep banks. Deep water means that light struggles to reach the riverbed, hence plants don't grow mid-stream, hence a lack of in-stream habitat, hence reduced carrying capacity for fish and other species. In addition, the new weirs inhibited fish migration. This is belatedly being addressed by an ongoing project to build adequate fish passes (see the example at Bevere Lock, for example) and restore now-rare species such as the twaite shad.

The twentieth century saw increasing housing development on the flood plain, covering

Engineering work at Holt Fleet Lock.

the precious water-meadows. Demands on the Severn's flow for water extraction have increased; the river currently supplies water to six million people.

Invasive species

A cleaner Severn has inadvertently helped the proliferation of non-native, invasive flora and fauna. Himalayan balsam has large purple flowers, with explosive seed capsules which help it spread rapidly. Japanese Knotweed also grows fast, reaching nearly three metres in height, efficiently colonising the riverbank far into Wales; it is unmistakeable by its large triangular leaves, red zigzag stems and spikes of white flowers near the leaf base in late summer.

Non-native fish in the river include barbel and zander. North American mink, escaped from fur farms in the 1950s, have decimated water vole populations. Attempts to eradicate mink failed* but their numbers are now falling, due to aggressive competition from otters. Signal crayfish (escaped from farms in the 1970s) carry crayfish plague and are larger and more aggressive than our native white-clawed crayfish; they are causing a decline in the latter, but hungry otters helpfully regulate their populations.

Habitats

Naturalists accept that our rivers will never return to their fully natural state. They are most concerned about, and preoccupied with, loss of habitat *diversity*, trying to preserve or restore a range of different natural habitats. Outlined below are some of the Severn's classic wildlife habitats. Of course, these habitats aren't found in isolation, they physically overlap one another and are interconnected and interdependent.

Shallows and riffles

"Water crowfoot, whose white flowers bloom like a garland on the head of drowned Sabrina, is the commonest weed of the river, growing abundantly in the shallows of mid-stream."

Brian Waters, *Severn Stream*, 1949

The free-flowing nature of the Severn means that it has abundant, shallow and fast-flowing water. Water crowfoot, the attractive white-flowered plant described by Waters, takes root among the pebbles in this dynamic habitat and flowers in July and August, for example decorating the river from bank to bank in Bridgnorth. Damselflies and dragonflies perch on the flowers, giving mating displays and feeding on the freshwater invertebrates which take cover beneath the fronds. Other Severn plants, tolerant of fast flows, include perfoliate pondweed (found from

---

* A similar eradication project in the 1930s, to remove muskrat from the Severn, was successful.

Welshpool down) and fennel pondweed (from Arley down). The pebbles and stones on the riverbed provide cover for stonefly and mayfly larvae, whilst waterboatmen and water beetles thrive on the water's surface. Shallows and riffles are also the favoured habitat of dippers and grey wagtails, which feed upon invertebrate larvae.

Steep banks

The Severn has a diverse range of riverbank habitats. Steep banks are found on the outsides of bends where active erosion is occurring and have also been created artificially on the Severn Navigation. They are often colonised by a narrow fringe of emergent marginal plants such as purple loosestrife (tall with purple flowers) and the flowering rush (not a true rush; tall with bright pink flowers). Steep banks allow kingfishers and sand martins to dig out well-protected nest tunnels. Martins require large areas of bare bank to burrow fresh tunnels annually, as the old ones become cluttered with debris; examples of sand martin 'cities' can be seen alongside the river passing Welshpool and also lining the meanders approaching the Ironbridge Gorge.

Wet woodlands

Wet woodlands are found on poorly drained or seasonally flooded soils. Due to the difficulty of accessing or exploiting these spots, they can be some of our most untouched and natural woodlands. These secretive habitats are especially prevalent along the Severn Uplands, where the river braids around islands

Sand martin burrows below Welshpool.

or winds through tunnels of dense willow and alder growth. The Severn's wet woodlands are often 'carr'; this term refers to low-canopied and tangled growths of birch, willow and alder which have established themselves over marshy tussocks. The water beneath is often choked with dead wood, important for insects.

Water-meadows

Water-meadows are any grasslands alongside a river, but strictly speaking the term refers to land which is seasonally flooded, also known as flood-meadows or 'damp meadows'. These meadows are usually managed environments with controlled irrigation to increase agricultural productivity. Traditional 'ham' water-meadows along the Severn Vale, used for haymaking and grazing, have largely disappeared. Those which survive (such as Upton-upon-Severn Ham and Severn Ham) are precious habitats, far more diverse than land subject to modern practices such as fertilisers. Meadowsweet, meadow cranesbill, autumn crocus and water dropwort thrive on these fertile alluvium grasslands, which also support huge populations of visiting and over-wintering birds such as corn bunting, curlew, dunlins, golden plover, gulls, kestrel, lapwings, redshank, snipe and starlings. The birds feed on invertebrates like worms which are forced to the surface by the wet ground. Pitchcroft Racecourse in Worcester, regularly inundated during winter, provides an urban example of a water-meadow.

Tewkesbury Abbey across The Bloody Meadow.

Wetlands

Wetlands are any areas which are usually inundated by shallow water. Approaching 90% of the UK's wetlands and half of its reedbeds have been lost since 1945. Preserving the Severn's wetlands is essential; aside from their role as a habitat, they capture carbon, store floodwater and filter out pollutants. The Severn has limited, extensive wetlands left; wetland habitats are mostly restricted to a strip along the water's edge and some of the largest, such as Grimley Marsh near Bevere Lock, are artificially created from former gravel or clay pits. Rushes (true bulrush) and reeds (common reed and bur-reed) extend out into water up to a metre in depth. They shelter vulnerable water voles, are home to reed warblers and provide roosting sites for swallows and sand martins.

Tidal flats

These habitats are intertidal, meaning that they cover and uncover with the tide. They begin, of course, below Gloucester and extend to the Severn Bridges and beyond. There are three main types of tidal flats; mudflats, clean sands and muddy sands. The names are self-explanatory, but the distinctions between them are important as each type forms in different environmental conditions and provides a different habitat.

Mudflats form in the spots least affected by tidal flow, for example shores only covered by spring tides. Here, silt brought downriver by the Severn can settle undisturbed. This fine-grained silt* is favoured by mud-snails and worms, which are picked over by wading birds such as curlews, dunlins and knots.

Clean sands form in the most dynamic intertidal environments, where the Severn's continuous tidal flows prevent finer silts from settling. A classic example is the Noose, the vast sandflat approaching Sharpness. Clean sands have more limited species diversity, although crustaceans, molluscs and sand-hoppers are adapted to survive in these harsh conditions.

Muddy sands form at relatively sheltered spots in between the two, providing a habitat for lugworms and mussels.

Wildlife

Outlined below are a few highlights of the River Severn's diverse flora and fauna.

Otters

"Though the otter is seldom seen, he inhabits the entire course of the Severn from the source to the sea ... he has no enemies but man, and if one regrets that he is seldom seen, this elusiveness alone has ensured his survival among us."

Brian Waters, *Severn Stream*, 1949

Without irony, Waters goes on in his book to cheerfully recount endless tales of trapping and shooting these beautiful sleek creatures, for the apparent crime of inconveniencing anglers. Those otters which survived human predation on the Severn were subsequently exterminated by organochloride pesticides, introduced in the 1950s. However, a glimmer of hope for humanity is offered by the group of Welsh farmers who voluntarily ceased using the pesticides before they were made illegal (1966), ensuring that a small population of otters survived in the uppermost Severn valley. This was crucial in helping the creatures to re-establish themselves along the whole

Mudflats at Purton Ships' Graveyard.

* A deeply unpleasant surface for paddlers attempting to land.

A swimming lesson

"I packed up camp and was on the water by five; it was an idyllic summer morning with light mist slowly lifting from the water. I had only been on the river some twenty minutes when I noticed what I thought was a Roe deer drinking from a rock at the top of an eddy. Stopping to watch, I discovered that it was in fact, three otters. The largest took each of the smaller ones, in turn, by the scruff of the neck and proceeded to drag them into the water, occasionally ducking them under. The pups seemed distinctly unimpressed and made for the bank as soon as the adult let go. I watched for a further ten minutes and then paddled on.

On returning home, I read up on otter behaviour; what I had witnessed was a swimming lesson. Otter pups are not instinctive swimmers at birth and have to be taught. At three months old, adults take them to the water for swimming and diving practice. The lessons continue until the young otters become proficient enough to hunt on their own."

Bill Taylor

river, beginning in the late 1970s when there were zero otters on the Middle Severn and Severn Vale. At the start of the twenty-first century, a study measured the proportion of potential otter sites in use; 100% on the Severn Uplands, 62% on the Middle Severn and 17% on the Severn Vale.

Otters continue to return to the river, with beneficial side-effects such as reduced mink populations. They are less likely to be encountered on sparse, tree-less stretches, such as that around the Vyrnwy confluence (planting is underway to rectify this), favouring the roots of ash and sycamore for their cavernous riverbank holts. They are widely spaced, ranging up to 40km along the river. They are most active at dusk or dawn, although the author has encountered one swimming in daytime. Their spraint (dung) is the biggest clue to their presence, a 3–10 cm sweet-smelling turd with scale and fish bones visible.

Club-tailed dragonfly by Charles Sharp.

Photo | Wikimedia Commons.

Dragonflies and damselflies

These wonderfully iridescent insects flit along wide, shallow parts of the Severn. How to tell them apart? Dragonflies are chunkier, have short bodies and keep their wings outstretched. Damselflies have extremely long and narrow bodies and fold their wings back. The club-tailed dragonfly, notably large with a 64mm wingspan, has its national stronghold along the Severn in Shropshire and Worcestershire. It is seen on the wing from late May to early July.

Dragonflies and damselflies have an extraordinary life cycle. After mating, the female lays eggs in shallow water near the river's edge. The eggs hatch (synchronously) and the larvae burrow into silt on the riverbed. After three to five years of living underwater, the insect crawls out of the water onto reeds to undergo partial metamorphosis into adult fliers.

Common Pipistrelles

If you are still paddling the Severn after sunset, you have a good chance of seeing pipistrelles hunting, swooping silently beneath bridges and dipping low across the water. Our smallest and most populous bat, it has a 20–23cm wingspan and weighs just three to eight grams. Because of their habit of hunting for insects over rivers and lakes, they are sometimes known as 'water bats'; a pipistrelle can catch several thousand insects in one night, using echolocation. Pipistrelles roost in tree holes and crevices; they are well established under the bridges along the Montgomery Canal. They hibernate from November but are the only bat species to fly in winter, emerging on warm days when their energy reserves are short.

Trees

Willow and alder predominate along the Severn's banks. These trees establish themselves easily when other tree cover is removed; crack willow, for example, is able to colonise new areas of riverbank by releasing cuttings which are carried downstream by flood water. Crack willow has oval leaves and osier willow has narrow leaves. Willow was cultivated on an industrial scale, by pollarding (cutting back to encourage growth); brittle crack willow for fencing and pliable osier willow for basket-weaving. The willow is usually accompanied by alder (known locally as 'walla'), and these now-unmanaged trees form extensive wet woodland habitats along the Severn Uplands. A study of the Severn Uplands found that where tree cover has been cleared (usually for farmland), the river banks are 20% wider and far more subject to erosion. The resulting slower flow leads to silt settling over salmon redds and mussel banks.

Enclaves of oak and ash survive along the banks of the Middle Severn, worthy of note as these scattered deciduous woodlands are remnants of the cleared forests which once extended between the Severn and Wye. Wyre Forest is the largest survival of this, alongside the Severn.

Birds

"Sandpipers whistled shrilly as they swerved off at our coming; curlew bubbled and called over quiet fields. It was most noticeable how very tame the river birds were along this deserted stretch. More than once, curlew (usually so very wild) let us get within five or six yards of them before taking to their wings."

Geoffrey Boumphrey, *Down River*, 1936
Boumphrey was paddling between the islands and undamaged oxbow lakes which are now Dolydd Hafren nature reserve. The Severn

Geese at Bridgnorth.

Heron at Shrewsbury.

Uplands' flood plains are visited by dunlin, golden plover and curlew in summer. A wide diversity of species thrive along the secluded valley of the Middle Severn below Ironbridge, especially wildfowl; Canada goose, goosander, mallard, mandarin, pochard. Many nest on the banks, below vegetation cover, whilst riverside ledges or buildings are favoured by species such as pied wagtails, who forage for insects along the river edge. There is less diversity on the Navigation below Stourport, although Worcester perhaps has the freshwater Severn's largest mute white swan population. The Severn Estuary has an extraordinary wealth of bird wildlife, recognised as an internationally important habitat for swans, ducks and waders; the RSPB estimate that around 74,000 birds annually winter here.

Wagtails and dippers

The white water in the Cambrian Mountains is favoured by dipper and grey wagtails, which feed on invertebrate larvae in the riverbed. Dippers (sometimes known as 'water ouzels' in the Midlands) hunt in clear, fast-flowing water by walking along the riverbed, overturning stones. Their dome-shaped nests are often located beneath bridges. Grey wagtails (whose numbers have been impacted by acidification) like riffles and weirs, utilising ledges and crevices for nesting. Their range extends much further downstream than the dippers.

Herons

Herons (colloquially called 'franks', after their call) are found all along the Severn. Although ninety centimetres tall, their white undersides and blue-grey backs seem to blend into any background. They stand motionless over eddy-lines, before revealing themselves by taking off with their distinctive slow flapping. Heronries (breeding grounds) are found in treetops and reed beds.

Kingfishers

"Before I was out of earshot of the weir its muffled roar was broken by a low-pitched squeak, something between the squeal of a mouse and the mew of a cat; the most vivid and glorious of all our birds has the meanest and most insignificant

cry of them all. I turned to see a kingfisher dart against the red face of the river cliff, until he alighted on the bare twig of a bush, resting like a jewelled sapphire against the red damask of the earth."

Brian Waters, *Severn Stream*, 1949

Waters' experience at Lincomb Weir is a (joyous) commonplace occurrence for paddlers along the length of the Severn. Kingfishers (sometimes known as 'dippers' in Shropshire) nest in excavated riverbank holes, but regularly reveal themselves (they are not exactly camouflaged) when they flit with improbable speed along the banks or across the river. A much rarer sight is their headfirst plunge into the water, where they catch a fish in their bill and swallow it whole. The author is yet to experience this, will you be luckier?

Fish

"If ever the day comes when a year has passed in which no salmon has been seen to leap in the Severn, or the horde of elvers turns aside at the mouth of the river, then Britain will have destroyed without redemption part of her heritage."

Brian Waters, *Severn Stream*, 1949

The Severn is home to pretty much every species of fish found in British rivers, some being native and others introduced; for example barbel, bream, chub, lamprey, pike, roach, salmon, trout and zander are commonly caught. The twaite shad is now rare, but projects are underway to restore it to the river. Fish populations* declined after the Navigation was engineered, and continued to fall for a range of factors, most notably pollution. 30,000 salmon were caught in 1885, but only 3,900 in 1970.

Eels and elvers

Elvers are young eels, translucent and around 7.5cm long. They arrive at our shores from February to May, following an epic two- or three-year and 3,000+-mile swim from their Atlantic spawning grounds in the Sargasso Sea. They swim upriver in vast numbers during nighttime spring tides. Elvers have been fished for centuries downstream of Tewkesbury, caught by nets on the estuary and box-traps upriver. 20-30 million were caught annually above Gloucester, before Maisemore and Llanthony Weirs blocked passage. Inevitably, the populations crashed and the European eel is now critically endangered; 'No elver fishing' signs now line the Severn Vale. Just a few hundred fishermen are authorised to catch elvers, which sell for very high prices; subsequently attracting organised crime gangs who coordinate illegal fishing.

---

* Authorities regularly use the word 'stocks', as if the fish only exist to satisfy angling sport.

Reserves and sites

Below is a selection of sites along the Severn which have been preserved or restored, representing a range of habitats.

Pwll Penarth Nature Reserve SO 139 926 – wetlands beside the portage around Penarth Weir (downstream of Newtown), reclaimed from sewage works. Gravel 'cliffs' have been created for wading birds to nest undisturbed.

Dolydd Hafren nature reserve SJ 208 004 – downstream of Caerhowell Bridge. Open flood plain with un-engineered meanders, islands and oxbows, rare on a major UK river! Habitats include shingle banks, water-meadows, wetland reedbeds and wet woodland of scrub and willow. Bird highlights include year-round waders and ducks, little ringed plover and yellow wagtail in summer.

Severn Valley Country Park SO 748 839 – a 51-hectare public space near Highley, created from a regreened area of mining waste. Coppiced woodlands along the Severn's banks.

Severn Ham SSSI SO 885 325 – the island between the Severn and Tewkesbury. Common land, one of the last few traditionally-managed water-meadows. The Ham is grazed in winter and the hay auctioned by July 12th, then the grass is left for another month before 'Aftermath' when it is auctioned again. Reed buntings present. The only breeding site of corn buntings in the region.

Coombe Hill Canal and Meadows Nature Reserve SO 847 263 – water-meadows and wetlands along the disused canal which joins below Tewkesbury. Dragonflies and damselflies in summer. Visited by huge numbers of wading birds in winter.

Slimbridge Wetland Centre SO 722 048 – 800 hectares of reclaimed wetland near Sharpness, visited by 30,000 wintering birds.

The Severn Estuary Ramsar – the entire tidal Severn from Frampton-on-Severn to the Severn Bridges, extending further still along the Bristol Channel's shores (16,942 hectares in total) is designated as a Ramsar site: a wetland of international importance. Habitats include tidal flats, wetlands and saltmarsh.

Further Reading

"You may leave the river, but the Severn will never let you go."

Brian Waters in *Portraits of Rivers*, 1953

Useful books

A Century of Bridges, Chris Witts, River Severn Publications, 1998, ISBN 0953271102

A Portrait of the Severn, Chris Morris, Tanner's Yard Press, 2006, ISBN 9780954209650

A Postcard from the Severn, Jan Dobrzynski and Keith Turner, The History Press Ltd, 2006, ISBN 9780750942225

Barges and Bargemen – a Social History of the Upper Severn Navigation 1660-1900, Barrie Trinder, Phillimore & co, 2017, ISBN 9781860777042

Ironbridge – History and Guide, Richard Hayman and Wendy Horton, Tempus, 1999, ISBN 0752414607

Marches, Andrew Allott, Collins, 2011, ISBN 9780007248162

Rivers and the British Landscape, Sue Owen et al, Carnegie, 2005, ISBN 9781859361207

Severn, Richard Hayman, Logaston Press, 2012, ISBN 9781906663667

Severn and Avon, Lawrence Garner, Landmark, 2008, ISBN 9781843063902

The Great Gloucestershire Flood 2007, Matt Holmes, Gloucestershire Media, 2007, ISBN 9780752445861

The Industrial Archaeology of Shropshire, Barrie Trinder, Logaston Press, 2016, ISBN 9781910839058

'The Most Extraordinary District in the World' – Ironbridge and Coalbrookdale, Barrie Trinder, The History Press, 2017, ISBN 9780750983693

The Nature of Central Wales, Fred Slater, Barracuda, 1990, ISBN 0860232751

The Nature of Worcestershire, G.H. Green and Brett Westwood, Barracuda, 1991, ISBN 0860234878

The River Severn, Keith Kissack, Terence Dalton Limited, 1982, ISBN 0861380045

The River Severn, a journey following the river from the estuary to its source, John Bradford, Hunt End Books, 2004, ISBN 9781858582733

The River Severn - a Pictorial History, Josephine Jeremiah, Phillimore & Co. Ltd, 1998, ISBN 9781860772719

The Severn Bore, Chris Witts, Amberley, 2011, ISBN 9781848689732

The Shropshire Severn, Richard K Morris, Shropshire Books, 1994, ISBN 9780903802611

The Welsh Border – Archaeology, History and Landscape, Trevor Rowley, Tempus, 2001, ISBN 075241917

The Welsh Marcher Lordships, Philip Hume, Logaston Press, 2021, ISBN 9781910839454

The Wildlife of Shropshire, Michael Leach, Shropshire Books, 1998, ISBN 0903802724

Welsh Borders, Christopher Somerville, George Philip Ltd, 1991, ISBN 0540012459

Wild Shropshire, Mark Sisson and Sarah Gibson, Nature Images, 2011, ISBN 9780957026506

Historical sources

A journey down the Severn is arguably enhanced by knowing what earlier folk experienced, and how they viewed the river. The following accounts are among those cited in this guidebook:

A Book of the Severn, A. G. Bradley, 1920

Camping by Water, Noel Carrington and Patricia Cavendish, 1950

Canoeing, William Bliss, 1934

Canoeing, W.G. Luscombe and L.J. Bird, 1948

Canoeing Waters, Percy Blandford, 1966

Down River, Geoffrey Boumphrey, 1936

Guide to the Waterways of the British Isles, British Canoe Union, 1936

Picturesque Views of the Severn, Thomas Harral, 1824

Portrait of the Severn, J.H.B. Peel, Robert Hale, 1968

Severn Stream, Brian Waters, 1949

Severn Tide, Brian Waters, 1947

The Book of Canoeing, Alec R. Ellis, 1935

The Diary of a Rowing Tour from Oxford to London, Howard Williams, 1875

The Heart of England by Waterway, William Bliss, 1933

The Rivers and Streams of England, Arthur Granville Bradley, 1909

Index

A

Aberbechan 72
Æthelflæd 125, 206
access 41
Alney Island 164, 166, 181
anglers 30
angling 23
Ap Gruffudd, Dafydd 89, 206
Ap Gruffudd, Llywelyn 72, 77, 206
Apley Forge 117
Apley Park 117
Apley Terrace 117
Arley Castle 127
Arlingham Peninsula 174, 175
Ashleworth Ham 163
Ashleworth Quay 161, 164
Ashleworth Tithe Barn 15, 164
Atcham 103
Atcham Bridge 15, 101, 105
Attingham Park 106
Attingham Park estate 13
Avon, River 156
Awre 181

B

barges 29
Battle of Shrewsbury 206
Battle of Upton-upon-Severn 155
Battle of Worcester 148
Bedlam Furnaces 118
Bevere Island (The Camp) 145
Bevere Lock 145
Bewdley 121, 123, 128, 129, 131, 133
Bewdley Bridge 129
Bewdley Museum 129
birds 222
Blackstone Rock 133
Blists Hill Victorian Town 118
Bore, predictions 182
Bore, surfing 183
Bore, the 172, 181
Bore, viewing 182
Breidden Hill 13, 86
bridges, safety 28
Bridgnorth 111, 112, 118, 121, 123, 128
Bridgnorth Bridge 112, 124
Bridgnorth Cliff Railway 123
Bridgnorth High Town 15
Brynderwen Bridge 72
Buildwas 102, 108
Buildwas Abbey 15, 108, 109
buoyancy 26
buoyancy aids 26
Burf, The 132, 135

C

Cadman, Robert 96
Caerhowel Bridge 69, 73, 75, 77
Caersws 63, 65
Cambrian Mountains 47
Camp, The (Bevere Island) 145
campsites 193
Canal & River Trust 30
canoes 23
Carreg Wen 204
Castle Meads 164
Castle Meads Bridge 167
cathedrals 207
Cefn Carnedd 204
Charles II 148, 155
Cilcewydd 76
Cil-Cewydd Bridge 75, 78
Cil Gwrgan Bridge 13, 69, 72
Clevelode 144
Cliff, The 163
climate 20
clothing 26
Clywedog, Llyn 20, 215
Coalbrookdale 113
Coalbrookdale Museum of Iron 118
Coalport 111, 112, 116
Coalport Bridge 112
Coalport China Museum 116, 118
Collow Pill 175
Coombe Hill Canal 163
Coombe Hill Canal and Meadows Nature Reserve 225
crayfish, signal 217
Cressage Bridge 102, 107
Crewgreen Bridge 84, 88
Criggion Quarry 86
Cromwell, Oliver 148, 155

D

Dale End Park 102, 109, 111, 118
damselflies 221
Darby III, Abraham 114, 119
Darwin, Charles 93
Davies, David 61, 64
Deerhurst 159, 162, 163
Diglis Basin 147
Diglis Dock 147
Diglis Lock 143, 148
Diglis Weir 147
dippers 223
Doctor's Field Countryside Heritage Site 93
Dolforwyn Castle 15, 72
Dolwen Bridge 57, 60
Dolydd Hafren nature reserve 13, 78, 225
dragonflies 221
Droitwich Barge Canal 145
drybags 25
Dudmaston Hall 125
Duke of Edinburgh's Award 34

E

East Channel 164, 165, 173
Edward I 72, 77, 206
eels 224
Elan Valley Aqueduct 127
elvers 224
emergency 30
Engine House Visitor Centre 126
English Civil War 148, 155, 208
entrapment 26
Environment Agency 30
environmental issues 215
equipment 26
Ermine Street 205
expeditions 32
Eymore Wood 127
Eytonrock 107

F

Felindre Bridge 54
Felindre Mill 27, 54
fennel pondweed 218
fish 224
fish weirs 208
flood-meadows 219
floods 213
flotation 26
flows 20
Folly Point Rapids 13, 38, 127
Forden Gaer Roman Fort 77
Fowler, Sir John 127, 210
Frampton Sand 175, 176
Frankwell Footbridge 91, 94
Fretherne 181

G

Garden Cliff 13, 174
Garthmyl 69, 73, 75
gauge, river level 31
gear, carrying 25
geology 201
Geufron 51, 53
Gloucester 161, 167, 169
Gloucester and Sharpness Canal 13, 41, 166, 177
Gloucester Docks 166, 177
Gloucester Life Museum 167
Gloucester Lock 166
Gloucestershire Wildlife Trust reserve 163
Glover, John William 95
Glover's Needle 146
Glyndwr, Owain 206
Glynhafren 53
Gwynne, John 96, 105, 146, 210

H

habitats 217
Hafren 21
Hafren Forest 13, 47, 215
Hampton 123, 125
Hampton Loade 121, 125
Hanley Castle 151, 153
Haughmond Abbey 104
Haw Bridge 161, 162
Hawford Junction 145
Hay Inclined Plane 116, 118
hazards 27
help, seeking 30
Henry IV 206
herons 223
Highley 123
Highley Station 126
High Rock 13, 118
High Town 118, 123
Himalayan balsam 217
Hock Cliff 13, 175
Holt Castle 144
Holt Fleet 131, 144
Holt Fleet Bridge 144
Holt Fleet Lock 132, 136, 141

I

Industrial Revolution 209
invasive species 217
Ironbridge 101, 102, 109, 111, 114
Ironbridge Gorge 13, 109, 113, 118
Ironbridge Gorge Museums 118
Iron Bridge, The 13, 113, 114, 209
Ironbridge World Heritage Site 119
Isle, The 13, 92
Ismore Coppice Wild Campground 103, 106

J

Jackfield 111, 112, 116
Jackfield and Coalport Memorial Bridge 111, 112, 116
Jackfield Rapids 13, 37, 115, 118
Jackfield Tile Museum 118
Japanese Knotweed 217

K

kayaks 23
Kempsey 143, 148
kingfishers 223
Kingsland Bridge 95

L

Lake Lapworth 203
Lake Vyrnwy 20, 215
launch points 187
Laundry Terrace 93
leashes, paddleboard 26
Leighton Bridge 76
Leighton Horseshoe 108
levels, water 31
licenses (waterway) 41
Lincomb Lock 13, 135
Little Shrawardine 88
Llandinam 57, 61, 63
Llandinam Bridge 58, 60, 63, 64
Llandrinio 87
Llandrinio Bridge 83, 87

Llanidloes 51, 55, 57, 59, 61
Llanthony Weir 27, 167
Llyn Clywedog 20, 215
locks 31
Long Bridge, Llanidloes 52, 55, 57, 59
Long Bridge, Newtown 67
Longney Crib 174
Longney Sands 13, 174
Long Reach 164
Lower Lode 152, 157, 159
Lower Lode Inn 151, 159
Lower Parting 167, 173
Low Town 123

M

Maisemore Bridge 161, 165, 169, 172, 173
Maisemore Ham 164
Maisemore Weir 27, 165
maps 39
Marcher lords 206
Melverley 97
Middle Point 176
Middle Severn 19
Mill Avon 156, 157
Minsterworth 174
mobile phone 27
monasteries 207
Montford 89
Montford Bridge 83, 84, 89, 91
Montgomery Canal 13, 73, 81
Montgomery, Roger de 206
mudflats 220
multi-day trips 33
Museum of the Gorge 113, 118
Mythe Bridge 155
Mythe, The 155

N

Nab, The 174
National Waterways Museum 167
nature reserves 225
Newnham 13, 169, 171, 174, 182, 183

Newtown 63, 66, 67, 59, 70
Noose, the 13, 175
North Quay, Worcester 147
Northwick Lido 141, 146

O

obstacles 28
Odda's Chapel 15, 163
Old Hall Bridge 51, 54
Ordnance Survey maps 39
otters 220
Over Bridge 173
Owen, Robert 67
Owen, Wilfred 97
Oxlease 164

P

paddleboards 24
paddlecraft 23
Penarth Weir 27, 71
Pendlestone Rock 13, 118
Pengwern Boathouse 95
Penson, Thomas 54, 55, 61, 72, 78, 210
Pepperpot Tower 154
Percy, Henry 206
phone, mobile 27
pipistrelles 222
Pitchcroft Recreation Ground 143, 146
Pixham 143, 149
playboating 38
playspots 38
Plynlimon 13, 18, 47, 49
pollution 216
Pool Quay 75, 76, 81, 83, 35
portaging 31
Port Ham 164
Powick Bridge 149
Powis Castle 15, 79
prehistory 203
Preston Boats Weir 13, 27, 104
Prince of Wales 77, 89, 206
Pritchard, Thomas Farnolls 114
Public Right of Navigation (PRN) 41

Purton Ships' Graveyard 176
Pwll Penarth Nature Reserve 71, 225

Q

Quarry Park 95
Quatford 13, 125

R

rapids 37
Red Lion 161
Redstone Rock 134
Rhaeadr Blaenhafren 48
Rhyd-esgyn 83
Rhydwhyman 77
River Avon 156
river level gauge 31
River Teme 148, 149
river users, other 29
River Vyrnwy 88, 97
Robertson, Paul (Cheesy) 184
Rodney's Pillar 13, 86
Romans, the 204
rowers 30
Ryall Wharf 155

S

Sabrina 21
safety 25
sand martins 218
Saxons, the 205
Seckley Wood 13
Severn Area Rescue Association (SARA) 30
Severn Bore Inn 174, 182, 183
Severn-Break-its-Neck Waterfall 49, 51
Severn Bridge Rapids 13
Severn Caravan Park 78
Severn Estuary Ramsar 225
Severn Ham 156, 225
Severn Navigation 41, 133
Severn Navigation, history 211
Severn Navigation, rules 29
Severn Park 112, 118, 121

Severn Porte Park 52, 57
Severn Stoke 141, 144, 151, 152
Severn Uplands 18
Severn Vale 20
Severn Valley Country Park 13, 126, 225
Severn Valley Railway 13, 128
Severn Way 38
Sharpness 169, 177
Sharpness Docks 177
Sharpness Lifeboat Station 171
Short Bridge, Llanidloes 55
Shrawardine 88
Shrewsbury 91, 94, 101, 103
Shrewsbury Castle 96
Shrewsbury Weir 27, 91, 103
signal crayfish 217
Slimbridge Wetland Centre 176, 225
Source, The 47
South Quay, Worcester 147
Staffordshire and Worcestershire Canal 137
Stanley 126
St Eata's Church 15, 105
St Mary's Church, Deerhurst 163
Stonebench 174, 182
Stourport 131, 132, 134
Stourport Basins 13, 137
St Peter's Church, Melverley 97
Strand 174
SUPs 24

T

Tar Tunnel 116, 118
Telford, Thomas 89, 97, 124, 129, 144, 155, 173, 179, 210
Teme, River 148, 149
Tewkesbury 151, 152, 156, 159
Tewkesbury Abbey 156
tidal flats 220
tides 182
Tithe Barn, Ashleworth 15, 164
Town Ham 164
Towpath Trusts 211
trees 222
trows 210
Tudor House Museum 154

U

Uffington 104
Upper Arley 123, 127
Upper Framilode 174
Upper Lode 155
Upper Lode Lock 13, 156, 157
Upper Lode Weir 156
Upper Parting 164
Upton Ham 154
Upton-upon-Severn 13, 151, 153

V

Victoria Bridge, Arley 127
Vikings, the 205
Viroconium 15, 107, 204
Vyrnwy, Lake 20, 215
Vyrnwy, River 88, 97

W, X

wagtails 223
Wainlode Hill 13
water crowfoot 217
water levels 31
water-meadows 219
Waterway Routes 39
Weir Head 84
weirs, safety 27
Welsh Bridge 94
Welshpool 79, 80
Wenlock Edge 13, 107
West Channel 164, 165
wetlands 219
Wharfage, Ironbridge 102, 111, 113
white water, grading 37
wildlife 215
willow 222
wind 29
Wingfield Arms 84
Worcester 143, 146
Worcester and Birmingham Canal 147
Worcester Bridge 143, 146, 147
Worcester Cathedral 15, 147
Wrekin, the 13, 107, 108
Wroxeter 106
Wroxeter Roman City 15, 107, 204
Wyre Forest 13, 127

Y, Z

Yew Tree Inn 159
Yr Allt Gethin 13

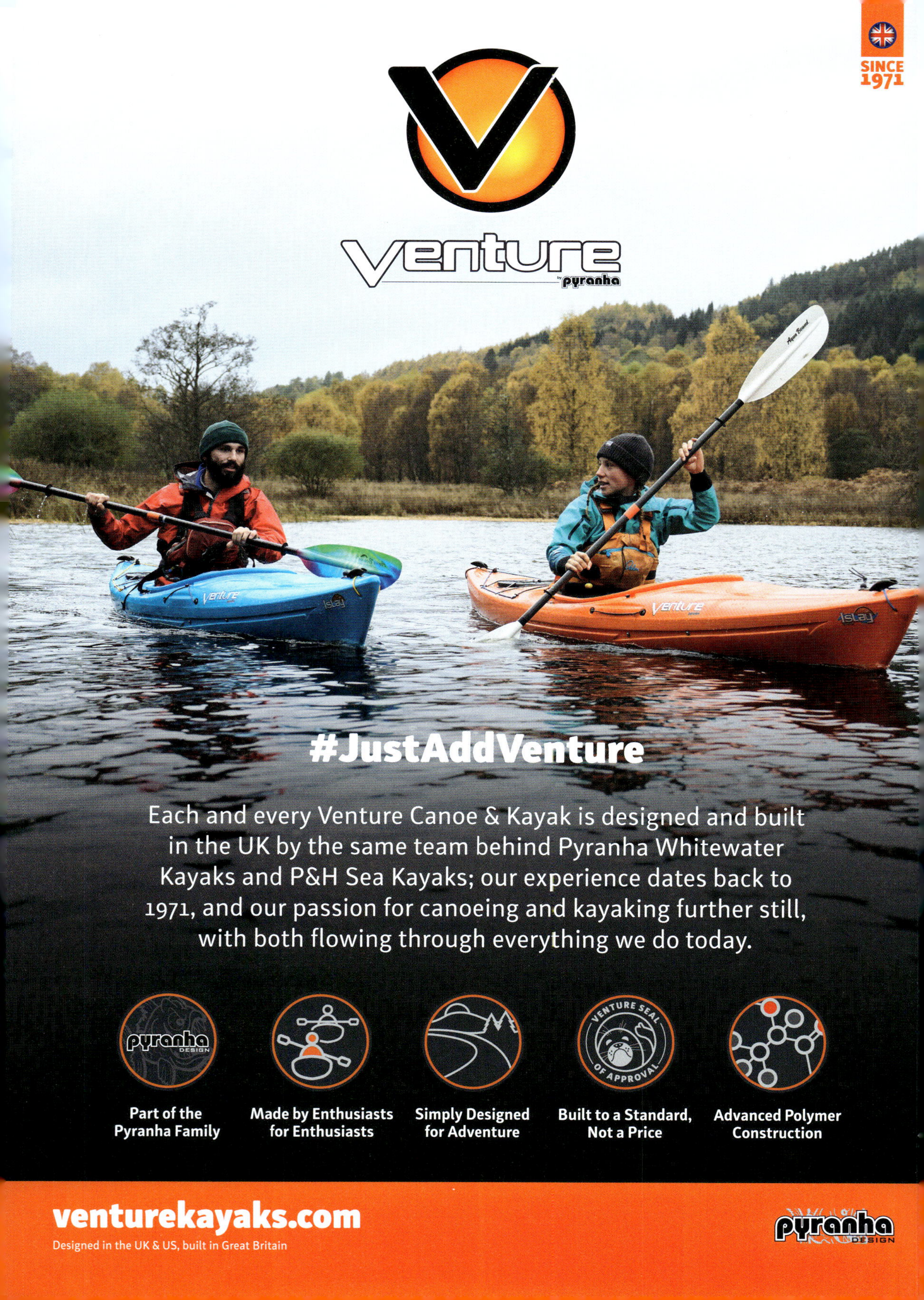

#JustAddVenture

Each and every Venture Canoe & Kayak is designed and built in the UK by the same team behind Pyranha Whitewater Kayaks and P&H Sea Kayaks; our experience dates back to 1971, and our passion for canoeing and kayaking further still, with both flowing through everything we do today.

Part of the Pyranha Family | **Made by Enthusiasts for Enthusiasts** | **Simply Designed for Adventure** | **Built to a Standard, Not a Price** | **Advanced Polymer Construction**

venturekayaks.com
Designed in the UK & US, built in Great Britain